PENGUIN BC

Salad

BIBLE

Salad

BIBLE

Jacki Passmore

Contents

Introduction

Salads have come a long way since the days of shredded iceberg lettuce with sliced cucumber and tomato. Today's salads are colourful, imaginative combinations of leafy greens, herbs, vegetables, meat and seafood. They can be cold and refreshing, or warmly satisfying. Vegetables may be raw and crisp, or grilled, roasted, steamed or marinated to introduce exciting flavours and textures. The addition of meat or seafood, bread or beans makes a salad substantial enough to enjoy as a main meal.

Dressings have certainly evolved from the old-fashioned combinations, like mayonnaise and lemon juice, that were once popular. Asian ingredients like soy sauce, lime juice, fish sauce and sesame oil add vibrant tastes and fragrances, while in Mediterranean salads balsamic takes the vinegar experience to new heights and fruity olive oils provide an aromatic and healthy alternative to vegetable oil.

Salad basics

There's nothing worse than a gritty salad, so make sure you wash all vegetables, leaves and herbs well before use. It's also important that ingredients are thoroughly dried after washing, otherwise the dressing will not coat them properly. A salad spinner is an essential tool, as it dries salad leaves and herbs thoroughly without bruising them. Spinners are generally inexpensive to buy, but if you don't have one, gently shake washed leaves in a clean tea towel to dry them.

Salad leaves are now available in stay-fresh packs, making it easy to have fresh salad ingredients on hand. (Some packaged salad mixes are pre-washed, others are not — check the label before using.) To keep unpackaged lettuce fresh, place it in a large plastic container with a draining rack inside and refrigerate. Wrap herbs in damp paper towels and they will stay fresh for a few days in the fridge.

Keep your pantry stocked with a range of vinegars and oils, and you'll be able to whip up dressings in minutes: balsamic, red and white wine vinegars, rice vinegar, and raspberry vinegar; fruity extra-virgin and light olive oils, as well as walnut, almond and sesame oils. Fresh is best, but bottled lime or lemon juice will suffice in an emergency, as will squeeze tubes of chopped herbs. I keep a few small screw-top jars in the cupboard for mixing and storing dressings — a few quick shakes and the ingredients form a beautiful creamy blend.

Some cooking terms you will come across in this book are defined below.

BLANCH: to briefly immerse an ingredient in boiling water to soften or very lightly cook it. Blanching brings out the bright colour of vegetables and retains their flavour.

REFRESH: to soak blanched or cooked vegetables in cold or iced water. This cools them, stops the cooking process and keeps them crisp.

PARBOIL: to boil vegetables until partly cooked (usually about half-cooked).

Leafy & vegetable salads

With such variety on offer – salad mixes (mesclun) of perky young leaves in all shades of green, soft oak leaf and mignonette lettuce, little gem cos, peppery watercress, and Asian greens like mizuna, shiso and tatsoi – leafy salads have never been more interesting. Bitter Mediterranean leaves like rocket, radicchio, treviso, witlof and endive add colour and pizzazz to the salad palate.

Crisp vegetables are the essence of a good salad, offering so many different flavours and textures. Raw beetroot has a deliciously earthy taste, fennel a delicate hint of liquorice, while cucumber and celery have crunch and are delightfully cooling. Cabbage, tomatoes and green beans are perennial favourites in the salad bowl, while mushrooms, bean sprouts and sprouted seeds bring their own unique flavours and textures to the mix.

< Avocado, corn & tomato salad
with chilli-lime dressing (page 6)

Avocado, corn & tomato salad with chilli-lime dressing

1 large avocado, diced

1 cup cooked or canned sweet corn kernels

½ cup diced celery or cucumber

12 small cherry tomatoes, halved

1 small white onion, finely chopped

2–3 tablespoons chopped fresh coriander, basil or mint

DRESSING

juice of 1 large lime

¼ cup light olive oil

1 small fresh hot red chilli, deseeded and finely chopped

1 teaspoon soft brown sugar

salt

Combine the avocado, corn, celery or cucumber, tomatoes, onion and herbs in a salad bowl.

Whisk the dressing ingredients in a small bowl, or shake in a screw-top jar, until sugar is dissolved.

Pour dressing over the salad, toss well and leave for at least 20 minutes before serving.

SERVES 4

Baby Asian greens & tofu
with mustard-sesame dressing

1 small bunch watercress

80 g baby bok choy or tatsoi
  leaves

80 g mizuna or wild rocket
  leaves

90 g bean sprouts, blanched and
  refreshed

4 plump radishes, thinly sliced

2 spring onions (white parts and
  8 cm of greens), sliced

180 g soft (silken) tofu, cut into
  1.5-cm cubes

DRESSING

1½ tablespoons Dijon or
  American-style mustard

⅓ cup light olive oil

1 tablespoon sesame oil

1 tablespoon fish sauce

1 tablespoon rice vinegar

1–2 teaspoons fresh lime juice

To make the dressing, whisk all ingredients in a small bowl or shake in a screw-top jar.

Snip the leafy tops from the watercress and combine in a bowl with the other greens, bean sprouts, radishes and spring onions. Add two-thirds of the dressing to the salad and toss lightly.

Pile the salad onto individual plates, add the cubes of tofu and drizzle the remaining dressing over.

SERVES 4

Beetroot salad

1 large fresh beetroot (about 500 g)

a handful of small beetroot leaves

1 small white onion or 2 spring onions,
  finely chopped

2 tablespoons mayonnaise (page 237)
  or sour cream

1–2 tablespoons fresh lime juice

salt and freshly ground black pepper

2–3 tablespoons chopped fresh dill
  or coriander

Wearing gloves to protect your hands from staining, peel the beetroot and then pass through the shredder attachment of a food processor (or use a mandolin slicer or sharp knife to shred it).

Combine the shredded beetroot with the beetroot leaves, onion, mayonnaise or sour cream, lime juice, salt and pepper and herbs and mix well.

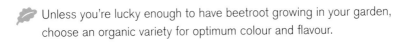 Unless you're lucky enough to have beetroot growing in your garden, choose an organic variety for optimum colour and flavour.

SERVES 4–5

Broccoli, zucchini & Swiss brown mushroom salad

⅓ cup raisins

½ white onion, sliced

2 tablespoons fresh lemon juice or white wine vinegar

1 cup small broccoli florets

1 cup sliced golden or green zucchini

1 cup sliced Swiss brown mushrooms

⅓ cup olive oil

freshly ground black pepper

2–3 tablespoons chopped walnuts, pecans or hazelnuts

Place raisins and onion in a large bowl, add the lemon juice or vinegar and leave to soak for 10 minutes.

Boil the broccoli in a saucepan of lightly salted water for 1 minute, then drain, refresh in iced water and drain again. Blanch the zucchini in lightly salted boiling water for 2 minutes, then drain and tip onto a plate to cool.

Put the mushrooms into the bowl with the raisins and onions. Add the olive oil, broccoli and zucchini, and salt and pepper to taste. Mix gently, then stir in the nuts.

 This salad can be made with cauliflower instead of broccoli: just boil the cauliflower for 2 minutes instead of 1 minute.

SERVES 3–4

Cabbage salad with walnuts & sour cream

250 g white cabbage, shredded

450 g red cabbage, shredded

½ bunch chives, chopped

½ cup sour cream or natural yoghurt

1–2 tablespoons cream

1½ tablespoons fresh lemon juice

salt and freshly ground black pepper

1 white onion, finely sliced

½ cup walnut pieces, chopped

If desired, soften the cabbage by blanching briefly in boiling water, then drain well.

In a large bowl mix together the chives, sour cream or yoghurt, cream and lemon juice, and season with salt and pepper. Add the cabbage and onion and stir until the dressing is evenly distributed. Cover and refrigerate for an hour or two.

Stir walnuts through the salad just before serving.

SERVES 6

Catalan salad of curly endive & almonds

¼ cup blanched almonds or hazelnuts

1–3 heads curly endive, depending on size

DRESSING

⅓ cup olive, walnut or almond oil

2½ tablespoons red wine vinegar or raspberry vinegar

2 cloves garlic, finely chopped

1 small fresh hot red chilli, deseeded and finely chopped

½ teaspoon sugar

salt and freshly ground black pepper

Preheat oven to 200°C. Toast the nuts on a tray in the oven for a few minutes, then set aside to cool.

Separate the curly endive into leaves and small clumps and place in a salad bowl.

For the dressing, whisk together the oil, vinegar, garlic, chilli and sugar, and season with salt and pepper. Pour dressing over the curly endive and toss gently.

Finely chop the nuts and scatter over the salad, again tossing lightly.

SERVES 4–6

Cauliflower & pumpkin salad with spicy coconut dressing

200 g butternut pumpkin, peeled and thinly sliced

12 green beans, cut in half

16 small cauliflower florets

120 g wombok (Chinese cabbage), shredded

8 snow peas, cut into strips

1 salad onion, finely sliced

1 fresh red chilli, deseeded and very finely sliced

2 tablespoons crushed roasted macadamias, peanuts or cashew nuts

a few sprigs fresh coriander or mint, for garnish

DRESSING

⅓ cup coconut cream

1½ tablespoons fish sauce

2 tablespoons fresh lime juice

1 tablespoon palm sugar or soft brown sugar

⅓–⅔ teaspoon sambal ulek or hot chilli paste

Steam the pumpkin for about 8 minutes, or cook in the microwave for about 3 minutes, until tender. Set aside to cool.

Bring a saucepan of lightly salted water to the boil and cook the beans for 2 minutes, then remove with a slotted spoon and refresh in a bowl of cold water. Add the cauliflower to the boiling water and cook for about 2 minutes, until tender but still a bit crisp, then transfer to the cold water. Add the cabbage and snow peas to the boiling water and stir until limp, then drain and add to the other cooling vegetables. ❯

Drain the cooled vegetables, then combine with the pumpkin, onion and chilli in a large bowl.

To make the dressing, whisk all ingredients together in a small bowl or shake in a screw-top jar. Pour the dressing over the salad and stir gently.

Transfer salad to serving bowls and garnish with the nuts and herbs.

SERVES 4–6

Char-grilled eggplant salad with tomato salsa

1 large eggplant

2 teaspoons salt

2 teaspoons ground cumin

⅓ cup vegetable oil

2 tablespoons sesame oil

200 g small leaf lettuce or rocket

24–30 black olives

fruity olive oil

SALSA

1 tablespoon soft brown sugar

2½ tablespoons fish sauce

2 large tomatoes, deseeded and finely diced

1 large salad onion, finely diced

1 small fresh hot red chilli, deseeded and finely chopped

2 cloves garlic, finely chopped

½ cup fresh basil leaves, chopped

½ cup fresh coriander leaves, chopped

freshly ground black pepper

Cut the eggplant into 1.5-cm slices and marinate with the salt, cumin, vegetable and sesame oils for 1 hour. Then transfer to a colander over a bowl and leave to drain for 20 minutes.

To make the tomato salsa, stir the sugar and fish sauce together in a small bowl until sugar is dissolved. Combine the tomatoes, onion, chilli, garlic and herbs in a salad bowl and add the sugar and fish sauce syrup and black pepper to taste. Mix well and set aside. ❯

Heat a heavy iron or non-stick pan over high heat, or heat a ribbed barbecue hotplate, and cook the eggplant slices for about 3 minutes on each side, until crisp on the surface and tender inside. Drain on paper towels until cool.

Pile lettuce onto individual serving plates, place two or three slices of eggplant on top and spoon some tomato salsa over the eggplant. Scatter black olives around the plate and add a drizzle of fruity olive oil.

SERVES 4 – 6

Cos lettuce & curly endive with gorgonzola & walnuts

½ cos lettuce or 2 little gem cos lettuces

2 loosely packed cups curly endive leaves

120–160 g gorgonzola or other strong
  blue cheese

½ cup chopped walnuts

salt and freshly ground black pepper

DRESSING

¼ cup walnut oil

2 teaspoons white wine vinegar

Place lettuce leaves and endive in a bowl, or arrange on four plates.

To make the dressing, combine walnut oil and vinegar. Drizzle a little over the salad leaves.

Cut the cheese into chunks and add to the salads, along with the walnuts. Season lightly with salt and pepper, and drizzle with more dressing.

SERVES 4

Cucumber, bean sprout & radish salad with orange-soy dressing

2 Lebanese cucumbers or
   1 continental cucumber

8-cm piece daikon (white
   radish) or 8–10 small radishes

⅓ punnet snow pea sprouts or
   other peppery sprouts, trimmed

1½ cups bean sprouts, blanched
   and refreshed

1 spring onion, finely sliced

DRESSING

zest and juice of 1 orange

1½ tablespoons light soy sauce

½ teaspoon sugar

1 teaspoon rice vinegar

white pepper or shichimi
   seasoning

Peel and deseed the cucumbers and cut into slender sticks.

Peel the daikon and cut into slender sticks. If using small radishes, trim the tips and tails and use whole, halved or sliced.

Toss cucumber, daikon or radishes, sprouts and spring onion in a bowl.

Combine the dressing ingredients in a small bowl or screw-top jar. Pour dressing over the salad and mix.

 Convert this salad into a main course by adding cubes of soft bean curd.

SERVES 4

Cucumber & seaweed salad

2 tablespoons dried wakame
  seaweed flakes

2 Lebanese cucumbers or
  1 continental cucumber

2 spring onions (white parts
  and 8 cm of greens), sliced

salt

2 tablespoons sesame oil

1¼ tablespoons light soy sauce

1¼ tablespoons rice vinegar

1½ teaspoons sugar

¼–½ teaspoon hot chilli flakes

Soak the wakame in cold water until it softens and expands.

Using a vegetable peeler or mandolin slicer, shave the cucumber into fine long strips, working around and discarding the seed core.

In a bowl, mix the cucumber strips, spring onions and drained seaweed.

To make the dressing, combine the sesame oil, soy sauce, vinegar, sugar and chilli flakes in a small bowl or screw-top jar.

Pour dressing over the salad, add salt to taste, mix well, then cover and chill for at least 20 minutes before serving.

SERVES 4

Dutch carrot salad
in creamy dressing

1 bunch Dutch (baby) carrots

½ cup mayonnaise (page 237)

1 tablespoon sour cream

½ teaspoon caraway seeds or
   ⅓ teaspoon lightly crushed
   fennel seeds

1 tablespoon chopped fresh parsley
   or mint

Trim roots and stems from carrots, scrub off skin with a clean kitchen scouring pad, then rinse. Cut larger carrots in half lengthways, then cut into 3-cm lengths.

In a salad bowl, mix the mayonnaise and sour cream with the caraway or fennel seeds and half the herbs. Add the carrots and stir until evenly coated.

Garnish with remaining chopped herbs.

SERVES 3–4

Escalivada (Spanish grilled capsicum & eggplant salad)

2 red capsicums

2 green capsicums

3 slender eggplants

1 × 200-g punnet large cherry tomatoes

olive oil

salt and freshly ground black pepper

red wine vinegar

chopped fresh mint or basil, to serve

Heat the barbecue to hot (or preheat the oven to 240°C). Place whole capsicums and eggplants on the barbecue (or on a rack over an oven tray lined with aluminium foil in the centre of the oven). Turn frequently until the outsides of the vegetables are completely blackened and soft to the touch. Remove, but leave barbecue or oven on. Place the grilled vegetables in a bowl and cover with cling wrap, then set aside for 10 minutes to allow the skins to loosen.

Put the tomatoes on the grill (or in the oven) and cook for 1½–2 minutes, until they have softened and the skins are blistered. Transfer to a serving platter.

Remove skins from the capsicums and eggplants. Cut capsicum into strips and eggplant into chunks. Arrange on the platter with the tomatoes. >

Drizzle salad generously with olive oil, season with salt and pepper, and sprinkle with some red wine vinegar. Garnish with chopped herbs. Serve warm, or chill and serve cold.

SERVES 4–6

Fennel & pecorino salad

1–2 fennel bulbs (about 300 g)
1 small head curly endive or coral lettuce
80–100 g pecorino cheese
1½ tablespoons fruity extra-virgin olive oil
2 teaspoons red wine vinegar
salt and freshly ground black pepper
a few sprigs fresh thyme and oregano

Trim the fennel, reserving the ferny fronds for garnish. Slice the fennel finely using a sharp knife, mandolin slicer or vegetable peeler.

Combine the fennel and endive or lettuce on a platter or in a shallow bowl and shave the pecorino over the top.

Drizzle on the oil and vinegar, season with salt and pepper, and garnish with fennel fronds and herbs.

SERVES 2–3

Gado gado vegetable salad

9–10 small potatoes

12 green beans (or 3 snake beans or 6 asparagus spears), cut into 5-cm pieces

1 carrot, peeled and sliced at a sharp angle

1 cup small broccoli or cauliflower florets

12 small snow peas or sugar snap peas

2 cups roughly chopped wombok (Chinese cabbage)

1 cup snow pea sprouts or other sprouts

spicy nut sauce (page 240)

1 small Lebanese cucumber, sliced

3 roma tomatoes, sliced

3 hard-boiled eggs (see note on page 69), cut into wedges

1 red onion, cut into rings

fresh herbs or shredded fresh red and green chilli, for garnish

6 lime wedges, to serve

Boil unpeeled potatoes until tender, drain, then cut each in half. In lightly salted water, parboil the beans or asparagus, carrot, and broccoli or cauliflower, then drain, refresh in cold water and drain again.

Boil more lightly salted water and blanch the snow peas or sugar snaps, cabbage and sprouts, then drain, refresh in iced water and drain again. >

In a large bowl, combine all the cooked ingredients. Add two-thirds of the spicy nut sauce and carefully stir it through.

Pile the salad on a platter and surround with the cucumber and tomato slices, and the egg wedges. Drizzle the remaining sauce over the top, then scatter with the onion rings and herbs or chilli. Place lime wedges around the edge of the plate.

SERVES 6

Gazpacho salad

3 vine-ripened tomatoes,
   deseeded and diced

1 red capsicum, diced

1 green capsicum, diced

2 Lebanese cucumbers or
   1 continental cucumber,
   deseeded and diced

1 large salad onion, diced

1–2 cloves garlic, very finely
   chopped

3 tablespoons chopped
   fresh parsley

2 tablespoons chopped
   fresh mint or basil

1½ tablespoons red wine
   vinegar

¼ cup fruity olive oil

salt and freshly ground
   black pepper

In a salad bowl, combine the tomatoes, capsicum, cucumber and onion. Add garlic, herbs, vinegar and olive oil and mix well. Season with salt and pepper.

Cover and refrigerate for a few hours before serving.

 Any leftovers can be whizzed in a blender to make a refreshing cold Gazpacho soup.

SERVES 6

Green beans with bacon, blue cheese & mustard dressing

250 g green beans, trimmed and cut in half

3 rashers shortcut bacon

80 g Roquefort or other blue cheese

a few sprigs flat-leaf parsley, for garnish

DRESSING

2 teaspoons red wine vinegar

2 teaspoons Dijon mustard

¼ cup walnut oil

salt and freshly ground black pepper

Boil the beans in lightly salted water for 3–4 minutes, until tender but still a little crisp. Drain and refresh in ice-cold water.

Cut the bacon into narrow strips and fry in a non-stick pan over high heat, without oil, until crisp. Set aside to cool. Crumble the cheese.

To make the mustard dressing, whisk the vinegar, mustard and oil in a small bowl, or shake in a screw-top jar, then season to taste with salt and pepper.

Drain the beans and dry in a clean tea towel. Toss beans with the dressing, bacon and cheese. Garnish with parsley.

SERVES 4–5

Green bean, tomato & herb salad

200 g green beans

4–5 roma tomatoes or a 200-g punnet of cherry tomatoes

½ cup fresh mint or basil leaves

1 × 400-g can kidney beans or mixed beans, rinsed and drained

½ white onion, finely sliced

2–3 tablespoons crumbled fetta or goat's cheese

2–3 anchovy fillets, finely chopped (optional)

DRESSING

¼ cup fruity olive oil

1 tablespoon white wine vinegar or 3 teaspoons balsamic vinegar

1 clove garlic, crushed

salt and freshly ground black pepper

Top and tail the green beans and cut in half. Parboil in lightly salted water for about 2 minutes, then drain, refresh in cold water and drain again.

Cut the tomatoes into wedges (or if using cherry tomatoes, cut larger ones in half). Tear or shred the larger mint or basil leaves. Spread the green beans and kidney beans over a platter and scatter the tomatoes, herbs and onion on top.

For the dressing, whisk the oil and vinegar in a small bowl with the garlic, salt and pepper, or shake in a screw-top jar. Drizzle dressing over the salad, then scatter with the cheese and anchovies (if using).

SERVES 4–5

Indian apple & potato salad

4 small potatoes

1 small red apple, finely sliced

½ green apple, coarsely grated

½ stalk celery, finely sliced

2 spring onions (white parts and 6 cm of greens), chopped

2–3 teaspoons finely shredded fresh mint leaves

DRESSING

1 teaspoon chaat masala

2 tablespoons vegetable oil

1½ tablespoons fresh lemon juice

½ teaspoon white sugar

salt and freshly ground black pepper

Boil the potatoes in salted water or steam until tender (about 10 minutes), then tip into a colander to drain and cool.

Thickly slice the cooled potatoes and combine in a bowl with the apple, celery and spring onions.

For the dressing, whisk together the chaat masala, oil, lemon juice and sugar in a small bowl, then season with salt and pepper.

Pour dressing over the salad. Add mint and stir carefully.

 Chaat masala gives a tangy taste to salads and side dishes. You can buy it from Asian spice sellers, or use sambar masala instead.

SERVES 4–6

Italian shredded carrot salad

4–5 carrots, peeled

1 red onion, sliced

30 small pitted black ligurian or kalamata olives

a few tiny sprigs fresh rosemary, oregano and thyme, leaves left whole or finely chopped

¼ cup fruity extra-virgin olive oil

4–5 teaspoons red wine vinegar

½ teaspoon crushed garlic

⅓ teaspoon crushed fresh red chilli

salt and freshly ground black pepper

Coarsely grate the carrots or pass them through the shredder attachment of a food processor.

To make the dressing, whisk the oil and vinegar in a medium-sized bowl, then whisk in the garlic and chilli and season with salt and pepper. Add the carrot, onion, olives and half the herbs to the bowl and mix well.

Serve the salad in small bowls, garnished with remaining herbs.

 If you can find blood carrots (dark-purple carrots with an earthy flavour), try them in this salad.

SERVES 4–6

Marinated capsicum & zucchini salad with olives

2 red capsicums

2 yellow capsicums

2 zucchinis

salt and freshly ground
  black pepper

olive oil

1 teaspoon cumin seeds

1–2 cloves garlic, finely chopped

balsamic vinegar

24 small pitted kalamata olives

1–2 tablespoons chopped
  flat-leaf parsley or basil

Preheat oven to 240°C. Place whole capsicums on a rack over an oven tray lined with aluminium foil and set in the centre of the oven. Roast for 15–20 minutes, turning frequently, until the skins are dark and the capsicums have collapsed. (Alternatively, you can place capsicums directly over a gas flame, and turn frequently until done.) Transfer the hot capsicums to a bowl, cover with cling wrap and leave to cool. (The trapped steam will loosen the skins.) Remove skins, then cut the flesh into strips.

Thinly slice the zucchinis lengthways. Brush with oil and cook in a non-stick frying pan or ridged iron pan over high heat until limp. Remove and leave to cool.

Combine capsicum and zucchini in a serving bowl. Season well with salt and pepper. >

Heat 1 tablespoon olive oil in a small non-stick pan and fry the cumin seeds until they are very fragrant and beginning to pop. Add garlic and cook very briefly, until fragrant but not browned. Tip into a bowl and stir in another 2–3 tablespoons olive oil and a good splash of balsamic vinegar. Mix well, then pour dressing over the capsicum and zucchini mix. Add olives and herbs and leave to marinate for at least 30 minutes before serving.

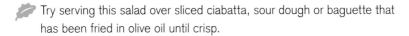 Try serving this salad over sliced ciabatta, sour dough or baguette that has been fried in olive oil until crisp.

SERVES 4

Mexican beetroot
& red cabbage salad

1 fresh beetroot (about 250 g)

½ yam bean or 8 radishes

300 g red cabbage, finely
shredded

1 red onion, sliced into rings

2–3 tablespoons currants or
chopped raisins

2–3 tablespoons roasted pepitas
(pumpkin seeds) or sunflower
kernels

1 large avocado, diced

a handful of peppery sprouts
such as onion, garlic or
mustard sprouts (optional)

DRESSING

5 tablespoons light olive oil

2 tablespoons red wine vinegar

2 tablespoons chopped fresh
mint or coriander

salt and freshly ground black
pepper

Peel the beetroot and yam bean and pass through the shredder attachment
of a food processor (or use a mandolin slicer or sharp knife to shred them
finely). Trim the tops and tails from the radishes (if using) and slice thinly.

Combine the beetroot, yam bean or radishes, cabbage and onion in a serving
bowl. Scatter the currants or chopped raisins, pepitas or sunflower kernels,
avocado and peppery sprouts on top.

Whisk together all dressing ingredients and pour over the salad.

SERVES 5–6

Mexican choko salad with herb dressing

2 chokos, peeled and stoned

1 cup fresh corn kernels

1 cup sliced green beans or celery

DRESSING

½ cup olive oil

2 tablespoons red wine vinegar

salt and freshly ground black pepper

2½ teaspoons chopped fresh oregano (or ½ teaspoon dried)

2½ teaspoons chopped fresh thyme (or ½ teaspoon dried)

3 tablespoons chopped fresh flat-leaf parsley

½ small salad onion, finely chopped

Cut the choko flesh into thick slices. Steam for about 8 minutes, until tender. Spread slices on a plate to cool.

Boil the corn and beans together in lightly salted water for about 2½ minutes, then drain, refresh in cold water and drain again. (If using celery, leave raw or blanch for about 40 seconds in boiling water.)

Transfer choko slices to a salad bowl and add the corn and beans or celery.

For the dressing, whisk the oil and vinegar together in a medium-sized bowl, then season with salt and pepper to taste. Stir in the herbs and onion. Pour the dressing over the salad and mix well.

SERVES 4–6

Mexican tomato & lettuce salad with avocado dressing

1 × 200-g punnet cherry tomatoes

1 × 200-g punnet yellow teardrop or grape tomatoes

2 large green tomatoes

2 witlof

1 small oak leaf or coral lettuce, or a curly endive

1 little gem cos lettuce or 120 g small salad leaves

2–3 small white pickling onions or 1 medium-sized red onion, cut into rings

¼ cup pepitas (pumpkin seeds), roasted or fried in oil

DRESSING

1 large avocado

1 tablespoon fresh lemon juice

2 tablespoons light olive oil

2 teaspoons mild or sweet chilli sauce

1 clove garlic, crushed

2 tablespoons chopped fresh coriander

sour cream (optional)

Cut the cherry and teardrop (or grape) tomatoes in half and place in a strainer over a bowl to collect their juices. Finely chop the green tomatoes and add to the strainer.

Spread the witlof and lettuce leaves on a platter and scatter the onions and tomatoes over (reserving the tomato juice).

To make the dressing, mash the avocado flesh in a small bowl. Add the reserved tomato liquid, plus the lemon juice, olive oil, chilli sauce, garlic and coriander and whisk until creamy. Add extra lemon juice if necessary, and enough water or sour cream to make a smooth, creamy dressing.

Spoon dressing over the salad and scatter on the pepitas.

SERVES 8

Mimosa salad

400 g iceberg lettuce

80 g baby spinach leaves

2½ tablespoons grain-mustard
 vinaigrette (page 243)

2 hard-boiled eggs (see note on page 69)

Coarsely chop or tear the iceberg lettuce and mix with the spinach leaves.
Toss with the dressing and pile onto small plates or tip into a serving bowl.

Peel the eggs and separate the whites from the yolks. Press whites through
a wire sieve and scatter over the salad, then press the yolks through the
sieve and scatter over the salad.

SERVES 3–4

Mixed sprout salad
with orange vinaigrette

2 punnets sprouts

½ punnet snow pea sprouts

1 spring onion, very finely sliced

juice and grated zest of ½ orange

2 tablespoons vinaigrette (page 243)

Use kitchen scissors or a sharp knife to trim the bases from the sprouts. Pull the sprouts apart in little tufts and mix with the spring onion and orange zest.

Mix orange juice into the vinaigrette and gently toss through the sprouts, using just enough dressing to moisten. Serve chilled.

Use a mixture of different sprouts including mild and peppery varieties. Sprouting your own grains and seeds at home is easy and rewarding.

SERVES 3–4

Mixed tomato salad with capers & basil

100 g yellow grape tomatoes

100 g baby roma tomatoes or large cherry tomatoes, halved

2–3 small hydroponic tomatoes, thickly sliced

¼ cup sun-dried tomatoes in oil

6 semi-dried tomatoes, cut in half

1 red onion, cut into thin wedges

1½ tablespoons drained capers

1½ tablespoons shredded fresh basil

½ tablespoon red wine vinegar

2 tablespoons fruity olive oil

⅓ teaspoon crushed fennel seeds

½ teaspoon crushed garlic

salt and freshly ground black pepper

Mix all the fresh tomatoes together in a serving bowl.

Drain the sun-dried tomatoes, reserving the oil in a small bowl, and chop them roughly. Add to the fresh tomatoes along with the semi-dried tomatoes, onion, capers and basil.

Mix the red wine vinegar and olive oil with the reserved oil from the sun-dried tomatoes, then whisk in the fennel seeds and garlic and season with salt and pepper.

Pour the dressing over the salad and toss gently.

SERVES 4–6

Mizuna salad with omelette strips

2 eggs

1 tablespoon chopped
fresh herbs

¼–½ teaspoon finely
chopped fresh red chilli

3 teaspoons fish sauce
or light soy sauce

1 tablespoon butter or oil

2 teaspoons sesame oil

2 teaspoons light olive oil
or salad oil

1½–2 teaspoons fresh lime
or lemon juice

salt and freshly ground black
pepper

100 g mizuna leaves or Asian
salad mix

a handful of shredded fresh
shiso, basil or mint leaves

a few sprigs fresh coriander,
for garnish

Beat the eggs with the chopped herbs, chilli and half the fish or soy sauce. Heat a tablespoon of butter or oil in a large non-stick pan and pour in half the egg mix. Cook until golden underneath, then turn and cook the other side. Slide out of the pan and roll up. Cook remaining mixture in the same way. Cut the egg rolls into thin slices, and uncurl into strips.

Combine the sesame oil and olive or salad oil with remaining fish or soy sauce, lime or lemon juice, and salt and pepper. Drizzle dressing over the salad leaves, add shredded herbs and omelette strips and mix. Garnish with coriander.

SERVES 2–3

Moroccan carrot salad

350 g carrots, peeled and cut into matchsticks

1 clove garlic, crushed

½ teaspoon harissa (optional)

⅓ teaspoon fennel or caraway seeds, crushed

¼ cup fruity olive oil

1 tablespoon fresh lemon juice

1 teaspoon cumin seeds

finely chopped fresh coriander, mint or parsley,
  to serve

Boil the carrots in lightly salted water for about 5 minutes, until tender but still a little crisp. Drain.

In the same pan, combine the garlic, harissa, fennel or caraway seeds and olive oil and cook gently until very fragrant. Return the carrots to the pan, add the lemon juice and stir. Transfer to a serving dish and set aside for about 10 minutes to cool to room temperature.

In a small dry pan toast the cumin seeds until they are very aromatic, then transfer to a mortar or spice grinder and grind to a powder.

To serve, sprinkle the ground cumin and fresh herbs over the carrots.

SERVES 4

New potato & dill salad

12–18 small new potatoes
(about 600 g)

1 small white onion, finely
chopped

2 spring onions, finely chopped

DRESSING

1 small bunch fresh dill,
chopped

2–3 tablespoons natural yoghurt

2–3 tablespoons sour cream

½ teaspoon dill, fennel
or caraway seeds

salt and freshly ground black
pepper

fresh lemon juice

Steam the potatoes or boil in lightly salted water until barely tender. Tip into a colander to drain. When cool enough to handle, cut each potato in half and place in a bowl with the white onion. Set aside until potatoes are completely cold.

Make the dressing by combining the fresh dill, yoghurt, sour cream and the seeds. Season to taste with salt and pepper and add a squeeze of lemon juice.

Stir the dressing and spring onions through the cooled potatoes, then chill for 15 minutes before serving.

SERVES 4–6

Persian fetta toasts with rocket, black olives & artichoke hearts

4 thin slices baguette, cut at an extreme angle

2–3 cubes Persian fetta cheese in oil

12 small marinated black olives

3 marinated artichoke hearts, cut in half

3 semi-dried tomatoes, cut in half

100 g wild rocket

balsamic vinegar

Grill or oven-dry the baguette slices.

Mash the fetta with a little of its oil, then spread over the toasts.

Arrange the toasts with the olives, artichoke hearts, semi-dried tomatoes and rocket on individual plates. Drizzle with balsamic vinegar and some of the oil from the fetta.

SERVES 2

Potato salad with beans
& anchovy-mustard dressing

3 large pink potatoes
  (about 600 g)

150 g green beans, sliced
  and blanched

1 salad onion, cut into
  thin wedges

a handful of chopped fresh
  basil, chives or parsley

DRESSING

30–50 g anchovy fillets, drained

2 teaspoons grainy mustard

2 tablespoons fresh lemon juice

2 tablespoons olive oil

3 tablespoons sour cream

freshly ground black pepper

Cut the potatoes into quarters and boil in lightly salted water until tender (about 12 minutes).

To make the dressing, mash the anchovies in a small bowl, then add the mustard, lemon juice, olive oil and sour cream. Whisk well and season with pepper. (The anchovies are very salty, so there's no need to add extra salt.)

Drain the potatoes and cut into bite-sized pieces while they are still hot. Add half the dressing and mix gently. Set aside to cool.

Once potatoes are cool, gently stir in the beans, onion, herbs and remaining dressing.

SERVES 4–6

Pumpkin & ricotta salad
with lemon & thyme vinaigrette

1 kg pumpkin

extra-virgin olive oil

salt flakes and freshly ground
   black pepper

3 cloves garlic, unpeeled

6 sprigs fresh thyme

2 sprigs fresh rosemary

180 g ricotta cheese

fresh lemon juice

Preheat oven to 190°C.

Peel and deseed the pumpkin and cut into 3-cm cubes. Line an oven dish
with baking paper and drizzle with oil. Add the pumpkin to the dish and stir
or toss until each piece is coated with oil. Season with salt and pepper, add
the garlic cloves, three sprigs of thyme and the rosemary. Bake for about
25 minutes, until tender, turning pumpkin pieces once or twice. Remove
from the oven and tip into a serving bowl, reserving the garlic cloves. Set
aside to cool.

When pumpkin is cool, crumble ricotta over it. Strip leaves from remaining
thyme sprigs and add to the salad. Season with more salt and pepper.

Squeeze the roasted garlic cloves from their skins into a small bowl. Add
a generous squeeze of lemon and 2–3 tablespoons olive oil. Whisk to a
creamy dressing, then drizzle it over the salad.

SERVES 4–6

Radicchio & endive salad
with crisp pancetta & Roquefort

1 small head radicchio

1 small curly endive

1–2 witlof

3 slices pancetta or bacon, cut into strips

90–120 g Roquefort cheese

fruity olive oil

raspberry, sherry or balsamic vinegar

Finely shred the radicchio and combine with the endive and witlof leaves in a salad bowl.

Heat a non-stick pan and fry the pancetta or bacon until crisp.

Cut or crumble the cheese into bite-sized pieces.

Jumble the pancetta and Roquefort through the salad leaves, adding a generous swirl of olive oil and a splash of vinegar.

SERVES 4–6

Rainbow capsicum salad

1 yellow capsicum

1 red capsicum

1 green capsicum

1 carrot, peeled

1 small cucumber

1 stalk celery, thinly sliced at an angle

1 salad onion, finely sliced

½ cup mixed chopped fresh herbs

1½ tablespoons sweet chilli sauce

3–4 tablespoons vinaigrette (page 243)

Cut the capsicums into long thin strips. Grate the carrot coarsely (or cut into matchsticks). Deseed the cucumber and cut flesh into fine sticks.

Mix the capsicum, carrot, cucumber, celery, onion and herbs in a bowl.

Combine the sweet chilli sauce with the vinaigrette and pour over the salad. Mix well.

SERVES 4–5

Roast pumpkin salad with grilled haloumi

1 kg pumpkin

olive oil

salt flakes and freshly ground black pepper

1 red onion, sliced

juice of 1 large lime

juice of ½ lemon

200 g haloumi cheese, cut into 2-cm cubes

2 tablespoons pepitas (pumpkin seeds), pine nuts or sunflower seeds

2–3 teaspoons finely chopped fresh oregano (or ¾ teaspoon dried)

2–3 teaspoons finely chopped fresh thyme (or ½ teaspoon dried)

2–3 teaspoons finely chopped fresh rosemary (or ½ teaspoon dried)

1 clove garlic, crushed

80 g rocket

Preheat oven to 200°C.

Peel the pumpkin or leave skin on, as preferred, then deseed, cut into 3-cm pieces and place on an oven tray. Drizzle with oil, toss to coat and season with salt and pepper. Bake for about 25 minutes, until just tender. Remove from the oven and leave to cool.

Soak the onion in the lime and lemon juice. ➤

Heat 1–2 tablespoons olive oil in a non-stick pan. Fry the haloumi with the seeds or pine nuts until the surface of the cheese has crisped. Add the herbs and garlic and fry briefly, stirring.

Place pumpkin in a salad bowl. Add the cheese and nut mixture (with its oil), along with the onion and its liquid, and the rocket leaves. Toss gently to combine.

SERVES 4–6

Rocket salad with avocado, blue cheese & pecans

120 g rocket

1 large avocado, cut into 2-cm cubes

1 tablespoon fresh lemon juice (or to taste)

2–3 tablespoons walnut oil

salt flakes and freshly ground black pepper

140–180 g soft blue cheese

½ cup pecans, coarsely chopped

Divide rocket leaves between four plates, or arrange on a serving platter. Scatter avocado cubes over the rocket and drizzle with lemon juice and walnut oil. Season with salt and pepper. Crumble blue cheese over the salad and add chopped pecans.

SERVES 4

Rocket with tomatoes, basil & shaved pecorino

120 g wild rocket

1 × 200-g punnet red or yellow cherry tomatoes

1 small bunch fresh basil

3 vine-ripened tomatoes, cut into narrow wedges

fruity extra-virgin olive oil

red wine vinegar

salt flakes and freshly ground black pepper

shaved pecorino or pepato cheese

Place rocket leaves in a salad bowl and scatter on the cherry tomatoes.

Strip basil leaves from the stems and tear larger leaves into pieces.

Add tomato wedges and basil to the salad and dress generously with olive oil and sparingly with red wine vinegar. Season with salt and pepper, scatter the cheese on top and toss lightly.

SERVES 4–6

Snake beans with crushed sesame seed & soy dressing

200–300 g snake beans

DRESSING

1½ tablespoons sesame seeds

1 tablespoon sesame oil

2 tablespoons salad oil

1 tablespoon light soy sauce

a squeeze of lemon juice

Cut the snake beans into 4-cm lengths. Boil in lightly salted water for 2–3 minutes, until tender but still a little crisp. Drain and refresh in ice-cold water.

To make the dressing, fry sesame seeds over medium-high heat for about 1 minute, until they smell toasty (be careful, as they burn easily). Grind the seeds coarsely in a mortar or spice grinder. Combine the oils and soy sauce in a small bowl, adding lemon juice to taste. Stir in the ground sesame seeds.

Drain the beans well, transfer to a bowl, then add dressing and toss.

 Try oven-roasted pumpkin done this way. You can substitute dukkah for the sesame seeds.

SERVES 4–5

Spicy egg, pea & corn salad

½ cup peas

½ cup corn kernels

6 hard-boiled eggs

1 Lebanese cucumber, diced

1 small salad onion, very finely chopped

¼ red capsicum or 1 large mild red chilli, deseeded and very finely chopped

2 tablespoons finely chopped fresh basil, coriander or Vietnamese mint

3 tablespoons mayonnaise (page 237)

2 tablespoons sour cream

2 tablespoons hot mango chutney or other fruit chutney

Bring a small saucepan of lightly salted water to the boil and cook the peas and corn together for about 3 minutes, then drain. Refresh in cold water.

Peel the eggs and chop flesh roughly. Drain the corn and peas. Combine the eggs, corn, peas, cucumber, onion, capsicum or chilli and most of the herbs in a serving bowl. Add the mayonnaise, sour cream and chutney and mix gently. Garnish with remaining herbs.

 To hard-boil eggs, place room-temperature eggs in a saucepan with enough cold water to cover. Bring slowly to the boil, then reduce heat and simmer for about 10 minutes. Drain and place in a bowl of cold water to cool.

SERVES 4–6

Spicy Indian chickpea & onion salad

2 large tomatoes

2 × 420-g cans chickpeas, rinsed and drained

1 onion, diced

½ stalk celery, diced

½ red capsicum, diced

½ green capsicum, diced

1 teaspoon finely chopped fresh ginger

1–2 teaspoons finely chopped fresh red chilli

1 teaspoon amchur (dried green mango powder), or fresh lemon juice to taste

¼ cup chopped fresh coriander

¼ cup light olive oil or salad oil

1 teaspoon ground cumin

salt and freshly ground black pepper

Cut the tomatoes in half and scoop the seeds and flesh into a sieve set over a bowl. Reserve the liquid and finely dice the tomato flesh.

Combine the chickpeas, diced tomato, onion, celery and capsicum in a serving bowl.

To the reserved tomato liquid, add ginger, chilli, amchur or lemon juice, coriander, oil, cumin, salt and pepper and mix well.

Stir the dressing through the salad and set aside for at least 30 minutes before serving, stirring occasionally.

SERVES 4–5

Spicy Indonesian rujak

3 thick slices sweet pineapple, cubed

2 lady's finger or sugar bananas, thinly sliced

1 nashi, Chinese or other firm pear, sliced

1 star fruit (carambola), sliced

1 Lebanese cucumber or ⅓ continental cucumber, sliced

½ stalk celery, sliced at an angle

½ red onion, sliced

1 spring onion (white and green parts), sliced

salt

¼ cup diced red capsicum or 1 fresh hot red chilli, chopped

¾ cup bean sprouts, blanched and drained

2 tablespoons chopped fresh coriander, mint or basil

lettuce leaves, to serve (optional)

DRESSING

2 tablespoons soft brown sugar

2–4 teaspoons fresh lime or lemon juice

2 teaspoons tamarind concentrate

3 teaspoons kecap manis (sweet soy sauce)

1½ tablespoons water

Mix the pineapple, banana, pear, star fruit, cucumber, celery, onion and spring onion in a salad bowl and sprinkle with salt.

To make the dressing, whisk the sugar, lime or lemon juice and tamarind in a small bowl with the kecap manis and water. ❯

Pour dressing over the salad, then add capsicum or chilli, bean sprouts and herbs and toss lightly.

Leave to marinate for about 20 minutes before serving in bowls or over lettuce leaves.

SERVES 4–6

Sweet & spicy pumpkin salad

600–750 g pumpkin, cut into bite-sized pieces

1 cup water

salt

3–4 tablespoons olive oil

2 cloves garlic, sliced

¼ cup cider vinegar

3 tablespoons soft brown sugar

½ teaspoon ground cumin

2-cm piece cinnamon stick

½ cup fresh mint leaves, roughly chopped

Heat a non-stick pan and add the pumpkin with 1 cup of water and a large pinch of salt. Cover and cook for about 6 minutes, shaking the pan occasionally. Drain off the water, add the oil and garlic, and cook over high heat until pumpkin is tender and caramelised on the outside. Transfer pumpkin to a salad bowl, then set aside to cool.

Add cider vinegar, sugar, cumin and cinnamon stick to the pan and simmer until syrupy. Remove cinnamon stick, then return pumpkin to the pan and toss just long enough to coat the pumpkin with the syrup. Tip pumpkin back into the bowl and toss with the mint leaves.

SERVES 4–6

Thai grilled eggplant salad

1 large eggplant (500–600 g)

¼ cup fresh lime juice

1 tablespoon fish sauce

3–4 teaspoons sugar

1 Lebanese cucumber, diced

2 spring onions (white and green parts), chopped

1 small fresh hot red chilli, deseeded and chopped

1 large fresh mild green chilli or ¼ green capsicum, deseeded and chopped

2–3 tablespoons chopped fresh coriander

2–3 tablespoons crushed peanuts or cashew nuts

Preheat oven to 220°C or grill to hot. Place the unpeeled eggplant in the oven or under the grill. (Alternatively, you can hold it directly over a gas flame.) Cook, turning often, until the skin is burned black and the eggplant is soft. Transfer to a glass bowl, cover with cling wrap and set aside for 10 minutes (the trapped steam will loosen the skin). When cool, peel the eggplant, cut the flesh into chunks, then drain in a colander.

In a salad bowl, mix the lime juice, fish sauce and sugar. Add the cucumber, spring onions (reserving some green tops for garnish), red chilli, green chilli or capsicum, and coriander and mix well. Add the eggplant and toss. Garnish the salad with nuts and reserved spring onion greens.

SERVES 4–6

Tofu & bean sprout salad with sweet & tangy dressing

250 g firm tofu

3 cups peanut oil or vegetable oil

½ cup finely sliced purple-skinned shallots or small onions

½ teaspoon blacan (shrimp paste) or 2 anchovy fillets, chopped

1 tablespoon tamarind concentrate

2 tablespoons sugar

½–1 teaspoon crushed fresh red chilli

1 teaspoon crushed garlic

1 tablespoon kecap manis (sweet soy sauce)

2 tablespoons cold water

250 g bean sprouts

4 spring onions or 1 white onion, finely shredded

Cut the tofu into 1.5-cm slices, then into bite-sized squares.

Heat the oil to very hot in a wok or deep pan, add the tofu and reduce heat a little. Fry tofu for about 3 minutes, until lightly coloured on the surface. Remove with a slotted spoon and place in a colander to drain and cool.

Add the sliced shallots or small onions to the oil and fry until brown and crisp. Remove and drain on paper towels. ❯

Pour off all but 2 tablespoons of the oil, then reheat the pan. Fry the blacan or anchovies briefly, then add the tamarind, sugar, chilli and garlic and stir-fry for about 40 seconds. Add kecap manis and 2 tablespoons cold water and simmer briefly. Pour sauce into a bowl large enough for the salad and leave to cool.

Blanch bean sprouts and spring onions very briefly, then drain and refresh in ice-cold water to restore their crispness. Drain well.

Add the tofu, bean sprouts and spring onions to the sauce and mix gently. Garnish with the fried shallots.

SERVES 4

Tunisian cauliflower & potato salad

3 pink pontiac potatoes

350 g cauliflower, cut into
small florets

a few sprigs fresh mint

24–30 small black pitted olives

DRESSING

1 teaspoon harissa

⅓ teaspoon fennel seeds,
crushed

¾ teaspoon ground cumin

¾ teaspoon ground coriander

grated zest and juice of
½ orange

4–5 tablespoons light olive oil

salt and freshly ground black
pepper

Boil potatoes in lightly salted water for about 8 minutes, until tender. Drain well. Boil the cauliflower florets for 3–4 minutes in lightly salted water, until cooked but still a bit crisp. Drain.

To make the dressing, whisk together the harissa, spices, orange zest and juice, and oil in a serving bowl. Season with salt and pepper. Add the cooked vegetables to the dressing, mix well and set aside to cool, stirring occasionally.

To serve, scatter the mint sprigs and olives over the salad.

SERVES 4–6

Watercress, mushroom & fennel salad

150 g watercress

120 g mixed lettuce leaves
(including baby radicchio
and curly endive)

1 small fennel bulb

½ cup finely sliced small
button mushrooms

1 large salad onion, sliced
into rings

DRESSING

5 tablespoons fruity extra-virgin
olive oil

1–2 teaspoons balsamic vinegar

3–4 teaspoons red wine vinegar

1 large clove garlic, crushed

salt flakes and freshly ground
black pepper

Combine the watercress and lettuce leaves in a bowl. Trim the fennel bulb to remove any discoloured parts, then shave finely with a vegetable peeler, mandolin or sharp knife.

Mix fennel, mushrooms and onion with the lettuce leaves.

To make the vinaigrette, whisk the oil, vinegars, garlic, a large pinch of salt and plenty of black pepper in a small bowl, or shake in a screw-top jar.

Drizzle the vinaigrette over the salad and toss lightly.

SERVES 4–5

Zesty mushroom salad with herbs

300 g button or Swiss brown mushrooms, sliced

juice and zest of ½ orange

juice and zest of ½ lemon

2 tablespoons light olive oil

2 spring onions (white parts and 8 cm greens), sliced

1 clove garlic, finely chopped

2–3 tablespoons chopped fresh basil

2–3 tablespoons chopped fresh parsley

1 tablespoon fresh thyme leaves

salt and freshly ground black pepper

Place mushrooms in a bowl and add the orange and lemon juice and zest and the oil, spring onions, garlic and herbs. Toss gently, and season to taste with salt and pepper.

For a crisp salad, serve at once. Alternatively, leave for a couple of hours to allow the oil and juices to soak in and soften the mushrooms.

SERVES 4

Zucchini & mushroom salad

1 zucchini, grated

4–5 button mushrooms
   or oyster mushrooms, thinly sliced

zest of ½ lemon

2–3 teaspoons fresh lemon juice

2 tablespoons fruity olive oil

1 tablespoon chopped fresh coriander,
   basil or flat-leaf parsley

salt and freshly ground black pepper

Combine the zucchini and mushrooms in a bowl. Stir in the lemon zest
and juice, olive oil and herbs. Season to taste with salt and pepper.

SERVES 2

Zucchini salad
with dill-yoghurt dressing

2–3 zucchinis (about 400 g)

2 tablespoons fresh dill tips

3 tablespoons natural yoghurt

1 tablespoon fresh lemon juice

1 teaspoon sugar

salt and freshly ground black pepper

a few mizuna or butter lettuce leaves

With a vegetable peeler, shave thin strips from the zucchini.

In a medium-sized bowl, combine the dill, yoghurt, lemon juice and sugar. Season to taste with salt and pepper, then add the zucchini and mix well. Set aside for about 10 minutes to allow the zucchini to soften.

Stir in the mizuna leaves, or serve the salad over butter lettuce leaves.

 Use a combination of green and gold zucchini for a more colourful salad.

SERVES 4

Meat & seafood salads

Turn a simple salad into a delicious, satisfying meal with the addition of ham, salami or bacon, cold poached chicken or veal, or leftovers from the family roast. Marinated vegetables, olives and salty fetta make great salad partners for cold meats, while fruit can make an unexpectedly delicious ally: try sweet cranberry dressing on a turkey salad, or use fresh fruit as a sweet and crunchy companion to rich meats like pork or duck.

Seafood salads and summer go together like champagne and oysters. Crabmeat, crayfish and bugs are luscious in salads, as are baby octopus, mussels, and prawns. Fresh salmon and tuna are at their best lightly poached or briefly seared on the outside and pink within. Freshness is paramount with seafood, so look for pink heads on prawns, bright eyes on whole fish, and a briny smell. Anything with a fishy odour is not fresh enough for a salad.

< Avocado seafood salad (page 90)

Avocado seafood salad

2 avocadoes

¼ cup diced cucumber or red capsicum

¼ cup chopped spring onions

2 tablespoons chopped fresh parsley or coriander

¾ cup small peeled cooked prawns

100 g cooked crabmeat, flaked

2 hard-boiled eggs (see note on page 69), chopped

lettuce, to serve (optional)

lemon wedges, to serve

DRESSING

2 tablespoons light olive oil

¼–½ teaspoon hot chilli sauce

2 tablespoons mayonnaise (page 237) or sour cream

1 tablespoon fresh lemon juice

Cut the avocadoes in half and discard the stones. Carefully scoop out the flesh without tearing the skins, which can be used for serving. Dice the flesh.

For the dressing, whisk the olive oil, chilli sauce, mayonnaise or sour cream and lemon juice in a large bowl. Add the cucumber or red capsicum to the dressing, along with the spring onions and herbs, then carefully stir in the prawns, crab, egg and avocado.

Spoon the salad into the avocado skins, or alternatively serve over lettuce leaves or shredded lettuce. Serve with lemon wedges on the side.

SERVES 4

Baby octopus & herb salad

1 kg cleaned baby octopus

3 teaspoons vinegar

1 cup water

a few sprigs fresh parsley

¼ cup olive oil

juice of 1 lemon

2 cloves garlic, finely chopped

⅓ teaspoon lightly crushed
  fennel seeds

salt flakes and freshly ground
  black pepper

1 cup mixed fresh herbs, leaves
  only (flat-leaf parsley, basil,
  chervil, dill, tarragon)

80 g small mixed salad leaves,
  coral lettuce or wild rocket

2–3 roma tomatoes, sliced

lemon wedges, to serve

Skin the octopus and cut out the eyes, if necessary. Rinse and place in a saucepan with the vinegar, 1 cup water and the parsley. Cover and cook on low heat for about 5 minutes, then remove from heat and leave to cool in the liquid. Drain, and cut larger pieces in half.

In a large bowl, combine the olive oil, lemon juice, garlic, fennel seeds, salt and pepper. Add the octopus and marinate for 10 minutes.

Mix herbs with the lettuce then toss the octopus and dressing through the salad leaves. Pile onto chilled plates, arrange sliced tomato on top and place lemon wedges on the side.

SERVES 4–6

Baby spinach & smoked trout salad with horseradish-cream dressing

4 large waxy potatoes

1 smoked trout

120 g baby spinach leaves

1 punnet snow pea sprouts

1 avocado, sliced

3 tablespoons sour cream

3 tablespoons mayonnaise

1 tablespoon horseradish cream

fresh lemon juice

salt and freshly ground black pepper

fresh chervil or dill sprigs, for garnish

lemon wedges, to serve

Boil the potatoes until tender, then drain and cut into bite-sized pieces. Flake the trout and remove bones. Remove any long stems from the spinach and trim the ends of the snow pea sprouts. Spread spinach and sprouts on individual plates or a serving platter, then scatter trout and avocado evenly over.

Mix the sour cream, mayonnaise and horseradish in a small bowl, and thin with a little cold water or light olive oil if necessary. Add a squeeze of lemon, and salt and pepper to taste. Spoon dressing over the salad, and garnish with the herbs and lemon wedges.

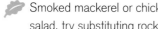 Smoked mackerel or chicken can be used instead of trout. For a spicier salad, try substituting rocket for the spinach, or watercress for the sprouts. The horseradish cream can be replaced with wasabi powder or paste.

SERVES 4

Bacon & egg salad with spinach

180 g baby spinach leaves

3 rashers short-cut bacon or 4 slices mild salami, diced

2 tablespoons light olive oil

3 hard-boiled eggs (see note on page 69), coarsely chopped

3 spring onions or 1 small salad onion, finely chopped

2 tablespoons sour cream

1 tablespoon mayonnaise (page 237)

2–3 teaspoons Dijon mustard

fresh lemon juice

Remove large stems from spinach. Cook the bacon or salami in the oil in a non-stick pan until crisp.

Combine spinach, egg and onion in a salad bowl.

Mix the cooked bacon and its cooking fat with the sour cream, mayonnaise, mustard and a squeeze of lemon juice, adding a little water if the mixture is too thick to pour.

Drizzle dressing over the salad, toss and serve at once.

SERVES 4

Buckwheat-noodle salad with chicken & ginger

1 × 250-g chicken breast

salt

⅓ teaspoon Sichuan peppercorns

1 star anise

1.5-cm piece fresh ginger

½ Lebanese cucumber, cut into matchsticks

½ red capsicum, cut into matchsticks

½ carrot, peeled and cut into matchsticks

soy and sesame dressing (page 239)

200 g buckwheat (soba) noodles

1–2 tablespoons sesame oil

3 spring onions (white parts and 8 cm of greens), sliced

1½ tablespoons shredded pickled ginger

2–3 teaspoons toasted sesame seeds

Place the chicken breast in a saucepan with enough water to just cover. Add a large pinch of salt, the peppercorns, star anise and ginger. Bring barely to the boil, reduce heat and simmer for 12–15 minutes, until the chicken is tender. Remove from the heat and leave to cool in the liquid.

Combine cucumber, capsicum and carrot in a bowl, add 2 tablespoons of the dressing and leave to marinate for 20 minutes.

Cook the noodles in boiling water for about 6 minutes, until tender. Drain and refresh in iced water. Drain again, add sesame oil and toss through.

Blanch the spring onions in boiling water, drain, then squeeze dry in paper towel. Set aside to cool.

Drain the cooled chicken and tear or cut into strips.

Combine the noodles, spring onions, chicken and marinated vegetables with the remaining dressing and the pickled ginger. Pile onto individual plates or into shallow bowls, sprinkle with the sesame seeds and serve.

SERVES 4 – 6

Bugs in a watercress, nectarine & avocado salad

2 bunches watercress

1–2 nectarines, pears or peaches

100 g mixed small salad leaves (mesclun)

100 g cherry tomatoes, halved

1 avocado, cubed

1 small salad onion, finely chopped

8 cooked Balmain or Moreton Bay bug tails

5 tablespoons vinaigrette (page 243)

Divide watercress into small sprigs. Slice the nectarines, pears or peaches (leave skin on).

In a serving bowl, mix the watercress, salad leaves, fruit, tomatoes, avocado and onion. Slice the flesh from the bug tails into medallions or chunks and toss through the salad with the vinaigrette.

SERVES 4

Chicken & celery salad with green grapes

350 g cooked chicken, diced

2 stalks celery, thinly sliced

2 tablespoons chopped fresh dill,
 parsley, coriander or mint

1 cup green grapes, cut in half

½ cup coleslaw dressing (page 237)

2 tablespoons thick cream

salt and freshly ground black pepper

Combine chicken, celery, herbs and grapes in a bowl.

Gently stir in the dressing, cream and seasonings. Chill before serving.

SERVES 3–4

Chicken salad with spicy sesame dressing

300 g roast chicken or turkey

1 large onion, finely sliced

100 g baby Asian greens

1 small bunch fresh coriander,
   broken into sprigs

DRESSING

2 tablespoons tahini

1 tablespoon sesame oil

2 teaspoons rice vinegar

½–1 teaspoon chilli oil

salt and freshly ground
   black pepper

Skin the chicken, if necessary, and shred the meat.

Blanch onion for 10 seconds, then drain and refresh in cold water, draining again when cool. Dry by twisting in a clean tea towel or squeezing between two sheets of paper towel.

To make the dressing, mix the tahini, sesame oil, rice vinegar, chilli oil, salt and pepper in a serving bowl. Add 2–3 tablespoons of cold water to make a thin sauce. Add the chicken and onion to the bowl and mix thoroughly.

Place Asian greens on individual plates and top with a mound of the chicken salad. Garnish with the coriander sprigs.

SERVES 3–6

Circassian chicken salad with walnut-cream sauce

2–3 chicken breasts (about 500 g)

1 bay leaf

1 small onion, cut in half and studded with 2 cloves

1 small sprig rosemary

2 small sprigs thyme

freshly ground black pepper

4–6 iceberg lettuce leaves, trimmed into cups

chopped fresh mint or coriander, for garnish

SAUCE

1 small onion, quartered

2 large cloves garlic, peeled

2 tablespoons unsalted butter, walnut oil or light olive oil

½ teaspoon hot paprika

2 slices bread, crusts removed

1 cup walnut pieces

½ cup blanched almonds

salt and freshly ground black pepper

Place the chicken breasts in a saucepan with the bay leaf, onion, rosemary and thyme and a big grind of black pepper. Add enough water to cover and place over high heat. Cover the pan and bring to the boil, then reduce to a simmer and cook gently for 20 minutes. Leave chicken to cool in the poaching liquid.

Drain cooled chicken, reserving 1 cup of the cooking liquid, then cut the chicken into bite-sized pieces. Cover and chill. **>**

For the sauce, place the onion and garlic in a food processor and chop reasonably finely. Heat the butter or oil in a small non-stick pan and cook the onion mixture for about 6 minutes, stirring frequently. Stir in the hot paprika. Set aside.

Moisten the bread with cold water, squeeze dry, then place in the food processor with the walnuts and almonds. Grind to a paste. Add the fried onion, half the reserved cooking liquid, and salt and pepper and pulse until the mixture is reasonably smooth, adding the remaining stock if needed.

Mix half of the nut sauce with the chicken and serve into lettuce cups. Spoon the remaining sauce on top. Finish with a drizzle of light olive oil or walnut oil, a sprinkle of paprika and a scattering of chopped mint or coriander.

SERVES 4–6

Corned beef & cabbage salad

200–250 g cold corned beef, sliced

1½ cups finely shredded white cabbage

1½ cups finely shredded wombok (Chinese cabbage)

½ cup finely shredded red cabbage

½ cup finely shredded radicchio

1 large red onion, very finely sliced

¾ cup coarsely grated carrot

1 cup coleslaw dressing (page 237)

½ teaspoon crushed fennel seeds (optional)

salt and freshly ground black pepper

fresh lemon juice

2–3 hard-boiled eggs (see note on page 69), cut into wedges

chopped garlic chives, parsley or spring onion greens, for garnish

Cut the sliced corned beef into 3-cm squares and set aside. In a large bowl, combine the shredded cabbage, radicchio, onion and carrot, mixing well.

To the dressing, add fennel seeds, salt and pepper and a big squeeze of lemon juice. Thin with a little water, if necessary. Add dressing to the salad and mix well. Just before serving, stir in the beef. Serve in a salad bowl or pile onto individual plates, garnishing with egg wedges and chopped herbs.

 Try using tangy sauerkraut instead of the radicchio or red cabbage.

SERVES 6

Crab & asparagus salad

120 g cooked crabmeat

6–8 asparagus spears

2 spring onions (white parts and 12 cm of greens), sliced

1 fresh red chilli, deseeded and cut into thin strips

a few small sprigs fresh coriander, mint, dill or chervil

¼ cup Vietnamese dressing (page 234)

1 tablespoon crushed roasted macadamia nuts

Pick over the crabmeat to remove any fragments of shell.

Bring a shallow pan of lightly salted water to the boil. Cook the asparagus for 1 minute until bright green, then drain and refresh in iced water. Drain again and slice thinly at an angle.

In a bowl, mix crabmeat, asparagus, spring onions, chilli and most of the herbs. Toss gently with the dressing, and pile onto plates or into bowls.

Garnish with the nuts and remaining herbs.

SERVES 2

Crab, prawn & celery salad

200 g cooked crabmeat

250 g small peeled cooked prawns

4 large stalks celery, finely sliced

1 small onion, finely chopped

DRESSING

½ cup mayonnaise (page 237)

2 tablespoons sour cream

1–2 tablespoons chopped fresh dill or parsley

fresh lemon juice

salt and freshly ground black pepper

Separate the crabmeat into bite-sized chunks and mix with the prawns, celery and onion.

Make a smooth, creamy dressing by mixing the mayonnaise, sour cream and dill or parsley with a squeeze of lemon juice and a little cold water, if needed. Season to taste with salt and pepper.

Fold dressing through the salad. Serve chilled.

SERVES 4–6

Crayfish with curly endive & lime mayonnaise

1 cooked crayfish or lobster tail (or 4–5 bug tails)

1 curly endive or coral lettuce

a few sprigs each of fresh chervil, dill and coriander

lime mayonnaise (page 237)

To remove the crayfish meat, cut along the edges of the under-shell with a short-bladed knife. Lift off the shell and ease out the tail meat. Cut the flesh into thin slices or chunks.

Pile greens and herbs onto plates and arrange the crayfish slices on top. Drizzle with lime mayonnaise.

SERVES 2–4

Grilled-squid noodle salad with spicy dressing

2 large squid hoods (tubes), cleaned

½ teaspoon crushed garlic

½ teaspoon crushed ginger

½ teaspoon crushed fresh chilli

1 tablespoon water

2–3 teaspoons fish sauce

150 g bean thread noodles

1 tablespoon peanut oil

chilli lime dressing (page 232)

1 salad onion, cut into thin wedges

3 spring onions, shredded

1 carrot, peeled and cut into matchsticks

1 red capsicum, cut into matchsticks

1 cup bean sprouts, blanched and refreshed

1 Lebanese cucumber or ⅓ continental cucumber, thinly sliced

¼ cup fresh basil leaves

¼ cup fresh coriander leaves

¼ cup fresh mint leaves

finely shredded fresh red chilli, for garnish

Slit open the squid and use a sharp knife to score the inner surface in a criss-cross of shallow cuts. Cut into 3-cm pieces and marinate for 20 minutes with the crushed garlic, ginger and chilli, 1 tablespoon water and the fish sauce.

Soak the bean thread noodles in hot water for about 12 minutes, to soften. >

Heat a heavy-based pan and brush with the peanut oil. Over very high heat, cook the squid for 40–60 seconds, turning and moving it constantly. The pieces should curl up and turn white. Remove and transfer to a bowl. Add half the dressing and set aside to cool.

In a salad bowl, combine the onions, carrot, capsicum, bean sprouts and cucumber. Tear any larger basil and mint leaves in half, then add most of the herbs to the salad.

Drain the noodles very thoroughly, then cut into 6-cm lengths. Add to the salad with the remaining dressing.

Pile salad onto plates and place a few curls of squid on each. Garnish with the remaining herbs and shredded chilli.

SERVES 4

Lemongrass beef salad

1 stalk lemongrass, trimmed and
roughly chopped

3 cloves garlic, peeled

1 fresh hot red chilli, deseeded

½–¾ teaspoon freshly ground
black pepper

2 tablespoons peanut oil

500–600 g beef sirloin or
fillet steak, fat trimmed

2 tablespoons fish sauce

2 tablespoons fresh lime juice

1½ tablespoons sugar

120 g mixed Asian lettuce leaves

leaves from 1 small bunch fresh
basil

leaves from 1 small bunch fresh
mint or coriander

In a mortar, spice grinder or blender grind the lemongrass, garlic, chilli, pepper and peanut oil to a paste. Spread some of the mixture over the steak, and set aside for a few minutes to allow the flavours to absorb. To the remainder of the mixture, add the fish sauce, lime juice and sugar, to make a dressing.

Heat a barbecue, non-stick pan or grill to hot, and grill the steak. Remove from the heat and let rest for 5 minutes, then cut into thin slices.

Toss the lettuce leaves and most of the herbs with a few teaspoons of the dressing and arrange on individual serving plates. Arrange the beef strips over the salad, drizzle on more dressing, and garnish with remaining herbs.

SERVES 4

Mexican tuna salad

450 g canned or cooked tuna

2 large tomatoes, deseeded and diced

1 onion, finely diced

1 jalapeño chilli, chopped

½ red capsicum, finely diced

½ yellow capsicum, finely diced

2 tablespoons drained capers, chopped

30 small black kalamata olives or 15 stuffed green olives, sliced

3 tablespoons chopped fresh basil or coriander

DRESSING

¼ cup fruity olive oil

fresh lime juice, to taste

salt and freshly ground black pepper

Drain the tuna (if using canned). Break tuna into chunks and place in a bowl. Add remaining salad ingredients and mix together.

For the dressing, whisk the oil, lime juice and salt and pepper in a small bowl, or shake in a screw-top jar. Pour it over the salad and toss gently.

 To add some extra crunch, rub thickly sliced ciabatta bread with a garlic clove that has been cut in half, then brush bread with olive oil and grill until crisp and smoky-tasting. Break into chunks and toss through the salad.

SERVES 4–6

Pastrami & beetroot salad with aioli

1 bunch baby beetroot

1 carrot, peeled

1 cucumber

4–5 radishes, sliced

4 large cherry tomatoes, halved

4 yellow teardrop tomatoes, halved

1 small salad onion, sliced

3 teaspoons fresh lemon juice

3 tablespoons classic aioli (page 233)

80 g mixed purple and green salad leaves, to serve

100 sliced pastrami, cut into strips

2–3 teaspoons chopped fresh chives, for garnish

Boil the unpeeled beetroot for about 20 minutes, until tender (or wrap in foil and bake at 180°C for about 45 minutes). Tip into a colander to cool.

With a vegetable peeler, shave thin strips from the carrot and unpeeled cucumber. Place strips in a salad bowl and add the radishes, tomatoes and onion. Wearing gloves to protect your hands from staining, peel the cooled beetroot and cut into halves or quarters. Add to the salad.

Stir the lemon juice into the aioli and thin with a tablespoon of cold water if needed. Drizzle most of the dressing over the salad and toss. Pile salad leaves onto plates, top with the beetroot mixture and arrange pastrami on top. Add remaining dressing and garnish with chives.

SERVES 4

Prawn & sweet potato salad with lemongrass vinaigrette

1 large sweet potato (about 750 g), peeled and cut into 2-cm cubes

2 tablespoons cashew nuts

4–5 tablespoons peanut or vegetable oil

1 large clove garlic, finely sliced

1 stalk lemongrass, trimmed and very finely sliced

250 g small peeled cooked prawns

2 spring onions (white parts and 15 cm of greens), shredded

60 g tatsoi or baby bok choy leaves

juice and zest of 1 large lime

salt and freshly ground black pepper

Steam sweet potato until tender (about 7 minutes). Set aside to cool.

Fry the cashew nuts in the oil until golden. Remove with a slotted spoon and set aside to cool. Add the garlic and lemongrass to the oil, then take off the heat and set aside to cool and infuse.

When everything has cooled, mix the sweet potato with the prawns, spring onions and tatsoi or bok choy in a serving bowl. Whisk the juice and zest of the lime into the infused oil and season generously. Pour dressing over the salad, add the cashews, stir carefully and serve.

SERVES 4–6

Roast beef & potato salad

2 large potatoes (about 400 g)

3–4 tablespoons grain-mustard vinaigrette (page 243)

1 small butter, oak leaf or mignonette lettuce

1 small onion, cut into rings

3 hard-boiled eggs (see note on page 69), cut into wedges

140 g cold roast beef, cut into strips

Cut unpeeled potatoes into chunks and steam or boil until tender (10–12 minutes). Drain well and tip into a bowl. While the potatoes are still hot, drizzle with half the dressing. Leave to cool.

Spread lettuce over individual plates and arrange potatoes, onion, eggs and beef strips on top. Drizzle with the remaining dressing.

 Try substituting cold corned beef or cold pickled pork for the roast beef.

SERVES 3–4

Roast pork & melon salad with ginger–hoisin dressing

300–400 g cold roast pork or cha siu (Chinese barbecued pork)

¼ rock melon

¼ honeydew melon

1–2 tablespoons pickled ginger

1 small bunch fresh coriander, separated into sprigs

DRESSING

2 tablespoons hoisin sauce

2–3 teaspoons light soy sauce or fish sauce

1 tablespoon very finely chopped spring onion

1 tablespoon liquid from pickled ginger (or use orange juice)

Slice the pork or cut it into chunks. Set aside.

Remove seeds from melons and cut into cubes or use a melon scoop to make small balls.

Mix pork, melon, pickled ginger and coriander sprigs in a serving bowl.

Make the dressing by combining the hoisin, soy sauce, spring onion and ginger liquid or orange juice. Drizzle dressing over the salad and mix lightly.

 Chinese roast duck can be used instead of pork in this recipe.

SERVES 4

Salami & tomato salad

250 g salami, sopressa or strasburg sausage

1 large tomato, roughly chopped

¾ cup diced fresh capsicum or ½ cup diced marinated capsicum

½ cup semi-dried tomatoes, chopped

½ cup marinated artichokes, chopped

1 spring onion, chopped

1 cup chopped flat-leaf parsley

DRESSING

2 teaspoons balsamic vinegar

2 tablespoons fruity extra-virgin olive oil

salt and freshly ground black pepper

Peel salami or sausage and cut into chunks (if using pre-sliced meat, cut into bite-sized pieces). Combine with all other salad ingredients in a serving bowl.

Whisk all the dressing ingredients together in a small bowl, or shake in a screw-top jar.

Drizzle dressing over the salad and mix well.

 To add some extra crunch, rub thickly sliced ciabatta bread with a garlic clove that has been cut in half, then brush with olive oil and grill until crisp and smoky-tasting. Break into chunks and stir through the salad.

SERVES 4–5

Seafood & fennel salad with dill dressing

12 mussels

2 tablespoons dry white wine

½ cup water

a few sprigs fresh dill

1 small fennel bulb

1½ tablespoons fresh lemon juice

5 tablespoons light olive oil

1 clove garlic, crushed

salt and freshly ground black pepper

2–3 tablespoons chopped fresh dill

6 large cooked prawns, peeled but tails left on

12 small marinated baby octopus, drained

3 slices smoked salmon, cut into strips

100 g mixed small salad leaves (mesclun) or 1 coral lettuce

lemon or lime wedges, for garnish

Place the mussels in a saucepan with the wine, water and dill sprigs. Cover and bring quickly to the boil, then steam the mussels for about 3 minutes. Remove from the heat and strain. Open mussel shells and run a sharp knife underneath the meat to remove it. Set aside to cool.

Use a vegetable peeler or mandolin to shave the fennel, or cut it into very fine slices with a sharp knife.

In a bowl large enough to hold the seafood, whisk the lemon juice and olive oil together until creamy, then add the garlic, salt and pepper and chopped dill and mix. ➤

Add the mussels, prawns, octopus, salmon and fennel to the bowl and mix well. Cover and chill for 10 minutes.

To serve, arrange mesclun or coral lettuce leaves on each plate and spoon the salad over. Garnish with lemon or lime wedges.

Use drained marinated mussels for a quick, economical alternative.

SERVES 6

Seared tuna with daikon & ponzu dressing

1 × 300-g square piece of tuna (or use salmon)

salt and white pepper

1 tablespoon grape seed oil or light olive oil

3 spring onions (green parts only), very finely sliced

15-cm piece daikon (white radish), grated

1 salad onion, grated

⅓ punnet peppery sprouts or baby shiso, for garnish

a few sprigs fresh dill, for garnish

1 tablespoon toasted sesame seeds

DRESSING

2 tablespoons fresh lemon juice

¼ cup light soy sauce

2 teaspoons rice vinegar

2 teaspoons mirin

⅓ teaspoon dashi stock granules (optional)

To make the Japanese ponzu dressing, combine all ingredients in a bowl. Leave for 1 hour before using.

Trim the sides of the tuna piece so that it is a neat square. Season lightly with salt and white pepper and brush with oil.

Heat a non-stick pan without oil and when very hot put in the tuna and sear on all sides until it is cooked to a depth of about 8 mm, with the centre still raw. Remove and let rest for 5–6 minutes. ➤

Blanch the spring onions in boiling water, then drain at once. Roll in a clean tea towel and squeeze dry.

Combine the daikon, salad onion and spring onions and pile onto four plates, reserving some for garnish. Slice the tuna and arrange on top. Drizzle with most of the ponzu dressing, then top with remaining radish and onion mix. Garnish with the sprouts or shiso and dill sprigs, sprinkle with sesame seeds and finish with a little extra dressing.

SERVES 4

Spanish ham salad with marinated capsicum & green beans

150 g green beans

250 g thickly sliced ham off the bone, cubed

120 g manchego, pecorino or other firm salty
  cheese, cubed

½ cup marinated red capsicum, chopped

½ cup semi-dried tomatoes, chopped

3 spring onions, thinly sliced on an angle

24–30 small pitted kalamata olives

3 tablespoons basil or rocket pesto (page 238)

Top and tail the beans, cut each in half and boil in lightly salted water
for 3–4 minutes. Drain and refresh quickly in iced water, then drain again.

Place beans in a bowl with ham, cheese, capsicum, tomatoes, spring
onions and olives and stir to combine. Stir pesto through the salad.

SERVES 4–6

Spicy Thai prawn salad

16–20 large cooked prawns, peeled and cut in half

lime and peanut dressing (page 234)

1 small salad onion, sliced

2 spring onions (white parts and 8 cm of greens), sliced

1 tablespoon very finely chopped lemongrass

2 teaspoons shredded fresh ginger

1–2 fresh red chillies, deseeded and shredded

½ cup fresh mint leaves

¼ cup fresh coriander leaves

3 leaves iceberg lettuce, finely shredded

1 large tomato, cut into wedges

½ small cucumber, deseeded and sliced

Place prawns in a dish with 2 tablespoons of the dressing and marinate for 30 minutes.

In a separate bowl mix the onions, lemongrass, ginger, chillies, herbs and lettuce. Cover and refrigerate for 20 minutes.

To serve, pile the salad onto serving plates or into bowls and add tomato wedges and sliced cucumber. Place the marinated prawns on top and spoon on extra dressing.

SERVES 4

Thai chicken salad

3 skinless chicken breasts (about 600 g)

1 red onion, finely sliced

2 spring onions (white parts and 12 cm of greens), chopped

1 bunch fresh coriander

1 bunch fresh mint

chilli lime dressing (page 232)

4–6 inner leaves of wombok (Chinese cabbage), trimmed into
cup shapes

2 tablespoons chopped roasted peanuts or macadamia nuts

Cut the chicken into 3-cm cubes and place in a saucepan with enough water to barely cover. Add a few pieces of onion and spring onion and some coriander sprigs. Cover and simmer gently for 12–15 minutes, until the chicken is cooked through. Remove from the heat and allow thechicken to cool in the liquid. Drain the cooled chicken and place in a food processor. Blitz to coarse crumbs, then tip into a bowl.

Strip leaves from the coriander and mint and chop roughly. In a bowl, mix the chicken with the herbs and remaining onions. Stir dressing through the salad. Serve in the wombok leaves (or on individual plates), and sprinkle on the roasted nuts.

SERVES 4–6

Tom's salad

1 tablespoon olive oil

4 rashers bacon

1 iceberg lettuce, chopped
or torn into small pieces

¼ large red capsicum, finely
sliced into long strips

1 carrot, peeled and grated

½ stalk celery, finely sliced

1 tomato, peeled, deseeded
and chopped

3 spring onions (white parts
only), finely sliced

40 g tasty cheese, cubed

2 hard-boiled eggs (see note
on page 69), chopped

vinaigrette (page 243)

Heat the olive oil in a non-stick pan, add the bacon and fry until crispy. Cool and drain bacon on paper towels, then cut into 1.5-cm × 2-cm pieces.

In a large bowl, combine the lettuce, capsicum, carrot, celery, tomato, bacon and spring onions. Mix thoroughly, then add the cheese and egg. Drizzle with the vinaigrette and toss lightly.

 This is a really versatile salad, because you can add, change or leave out ingredients as you like. For example, you can omit the eggs, or add nuts such as almonds or walnuts. For a more grown-up feel, substitute Persian fetta for the tasty cheese and add toasted pine nuts. Or add a cup of shredded cooked chicken to make a really substantial meal.

SERVES 4–6

Turkey salad with cranberry dressing

300 g cold roast turkey
1 spring onion, chopped
1 large avocado, cubed
¼ cup craisins (optional)
100 g wild rocket

DRESSING

¼ cup cranberry jelly
2 tablespoons fresh lemon juice
1 teaspoon honey
1 teaspoon sweet chilli sauce
1 tablespoon salad oil or light olive oil

Shred the roast turkey, or cut into 1.5-cm cubes.

To make the dressing, whisk together the cranberry jelly, lemon juice, honey, sweet chilli and oil.

In a medium-sized bowl, combine the turkey, spring onion, avocado and craisins (if using). Gently stir in the dressing.

Serve salad over rocket leaves.

 Craisins are sweetened dried cranberries. They have a tangy flavour and pleasant chewiness.

SERVES 4

Vietnamese cabbage & chicken salad

1 red onion, finely sliced

3 spring onions (white parts and 8 cm of greens)

2 cups shredded cooked chicken

1 carrot, peeled and grated

3 cups finely shredded wombok (Chinese cabbage)

1 cup finely shredded red or savoy cabbage

¾ cup bean sprouts

1 small bunch fresh Vietnamese mint, leaves chopped

1 small bunch fresh mint, leaves chopped

DRESSING

2 tablespoons golden syrup

¼ cup fish sauce

1 tablespoon water

½–1 fresh hot red chilli, finely chopped

1 tablespoon fresh lime juice or rice vinegar

2 cloves garlic, finely chopped

2 tablespoons peanut oil

To make the dressing, whisk together all ingredients in a large bowl. Add the sliced onion and mix well. Leave to marinate for 10 minutes.

Cut the spring onions into 4-cm pieces and shred finely lengthways. Combine in a bowl with the chicken, carrot, cabbage and sprouts. Add the dressing and marinated onions, along with the chopped herbs and toss to combine.

SERVES 4–6

Vietnamese roast pork salad wraps

80 g rice vermicelli

3 spring onions (white parts and 8 cm of greens), finely sliced at an angle

3 thin slices fresh ginger, shredded

1 stalk lemongrass, trimmed and very finely sliced

1 small bunch fresh mint or Vietnamese mint

1 small bunch fresh basil

1 small bunch fresh coriander

200 g cold roast pork, shredded

180 g bean sprouts, blanched and refreshed

1 Lebanese cucumber or ½ continental cucumber, sliced

½ red capsicum, cut into thin strips

1 large carrot, peeled and coarsely grated

1 tablespoon chopped roasted peanuts

Vietnamese dressing (page 234)

1 packet small rice paper wrappers (banh trang)

Soften the rice vermicelli in boiling water, then drain and leave to cool.

Combine spring onions with ginger and lemongrass. Strip the leaves from the herbs.

Pile each of the salad ingredients – rice vermicelli, spring onion mix, pork, sprouts, cucumber, capsicum, carrot and herbs – separately on a platter. Scatter roasted nuts over the salad. Pour salad dressing into a small serving bowl and place in the centre of the plate, along with a spoon.

Take the salad to the table along with a shallow bowl of hot water, the rice paper wrappers and a clean tea towel. To assemble, soften wrappers one by one in the hot water and pass to guests. Diners then place a portion of each of the salad components and a spoonful of the sauce in their wrapper and roll it up.

Alternatively, you can make up the wraps beforehand. Store them on a plate covered with a damp tea towel or cling wrap, so the rice paper doesn't dry out.

SERVES 6

Vitello tonnato (veal salad with creamy tuna sauce)

300–400 g cold roast or poached veal

1½ cups cooked sliced green beans
   or canned white beans, drained

1 × 185-g can tuna in oil

½ cup crème fraîche or sour cream

1 tablespoon fresh lemon juice

1 spring onion, chopped

2 sprigs fresh parsley

2 anchovies

60 g baby spinach or rocket leaves

Cut the cold veal into thin slices or bite-sized chunks and mix with the beans in a large bowl.

In a food processor or blender, place the tuna (with its oil), crème fraîche or sour cream, lemon juice, spring onion, parsley and anchovies, and purée.

Add the tuna sauce and spinach or rocket to the veal and bean mixture and stir to combine.

SERVES 4

Warm salads

Comfort food. Creative food. Food to tease the taste buds and capture the imagination. Warm salads provide satisfaction, variety and joyful juxtapositions.

Meat, seafood and vegetables, sizzling, smoky and charred from the barbecue or grill, draped over crisp and crunchy greens. Hot salty bacon wilting tender leaves. Roast vegetables glistening with olive oil. Explosions of flavour in the mouth — unexpected bursts of sweetness and tangy lemon contrasting with the crunchy surprise of nuts and seeds.

< Beef salad with soft brie
  & pancetta (page 142)

Beef salad with soft brie & pancetta

1 × 600–700-g piece beef eye
    fillet

1–2 cloves garlic, crushed

olive oil

salt and freshly ground black
    pepper

120–180 g mixed salad leaves

3 thin slices pancetta, cut into
    small strips

¼ cup pine nuts or slivered
    almonds

2 tablespoons balsamic vinegar

1 tablespoon fig jam
    or marmalade

1 wheel ripe brie, thickly sliced

Trim the eye fillet and rub all over with crushed garlic and olive oil, and season with salt and pepper. Heat a heavy frying pan to very hot, add the meat and roll it to sear on all sides. Watch the end of the meat to check how it is cooking – it should remain very rare in the centre. Remove from the pan and set aside to rest for 5–6 minutes.

Arrange the salad leaves on plates or spread over a platter.

Reheat the (unwashed) pan and add ⅓ cup olive oil. Fry the pancetta and nuts, scraping the bottom of the pan to incorporate any residue from the meat. Stir in the balsamic vinegar and jam or marmalade and mix well.

Slice the beef thinly and drape over the salad leaves. Spoon on the pancetta, nuts and dressing from the pan, then place slices of brie over the top.

SERVES 4–6

Cajun chicken salad

1 × 180-g chicken breast

1 tablespoon Cajun seasoning

olive oil

plain flour seasoned with salt
  and pepper, for coating

1 egg beaten with 1 tablespoon
  milk

fine dry breadcrumbs,
  for crumbing

inner leaves of 1 cos
  or mignonette lettuce

1 cup curly endive or coral
  lettuce leaves

1 small salad onion, finely sliced

3–4 teaspoons vinaigrette
  (page 243)

1 tablespoon tomato chutney
  or sweet chilli sauce

3 tablespoons sour cream

1 tomato, cut into wedges

¼ cucumber, finely sliced

Cut the chicken into slices about 1.5 cm thick. Combine the Cajun
seasoning with 2 tablespoons oil and brush evenly over the chicken.
Set aside for 20 minutes to marinate.

Lightly coat the chicken strips with flour, then dip into the egg and milk
mixture and coat with breadcrumbs. If time allows, chill for 20 minutes.

Heat a large non-stick pan and add ½ cup olive oil. Fry the crumbed
chicken strips until golden brown (about 2½ minutes), then drain well
on paper towels. ➤

Mix the lettuce leaves, endive and onion in a bowl and dress with the vinaigrette. Divide the salad between two plates. Stir chutney or sweet chilli into the sour cream.

Arrange chicken strips on the salad, add a dollop of the sour cream dressing and garnish with tomato wedges and cucumber slices.

SERVES 2

Char-grilled potatoes with spinach & aioli

3 pink pontiac potatoes
4 kipfler potatoes
olive oil
salt flakes
80 g baby spinach leaves
½ quantity classic aioli (page 233)

Scrub the pink potatoes, but leave unpeeled. Cut into 1-cm slices. Peel the kipflers and cut into 1-cm slices. Steam potatoes until almost cooked (about 8 minutes), then spread on paper towels to dry. Brush with olive oil and sprinkle with salt.

Heat a ribbed pan or hotplate over high heat and cook the potatoes until well branded with sear marks on both sides.

While the potatoes are grilling, remove any thick stems from the spinach and spread over a platter.

Whisk 1–2 tablespoons of water into the aioli, to make it smooth enough to drizzle over the salad.

Arrange the warm potatoes over the spinach and pour on the dressing.

SERVES 4–6

Grilled asparagus, fennel & zucchini salad

2 zucchinis

20 thin asparagus spears,
ends snapped off and cut
in half lengthways

2 small fennel bulbs or red
onions, cut into wedges

salt flakes

80–120 g mixed small salad
leaves (mesclun)

DRESSING

⅓ cup extra-virgin olive oil

3–4 teaspoons balsamic vinegar

1 clove garlic, crushed with
⅓ teaspoon salt

freshly ground black pepper

⅓ teaspoon finely chopped
fresh red chilli or chilli
flakes (optional)

Use a vegetable peeler to shave the zucchinis into long strips.

Brush all the vegetables with olive oil and cook on a hot ribbed pan until
scored with black sear marks and tender (3–4 minutes for zucchini, about
5 minutes for the asparagus, and 6–7 minutes for the fennel or onion).
Sprinkle with salt flakes.

Make the dressing by whisking all ingredients together.

Toss the salad leaves with some of the dressing, spread on a platter
and add the vegetables. Drizzle on remaining dressing.

SERVES 4–6

Mediterranean grilled quail salad

8 quails

4 slices pancetta

16 fresh sage leaves

salt and freshly ground black
pepper

olive oil

1 curly endive or coral lettuce

1 oak leaf, mignonette or baby
cos lettuce

8 marinated artichokes,
cut into quarters

2 tablespoons tapenade
(page 242)

3–4 tablespoons extra-virgin
olive oil

lemon wedges, for garnish

Rinse, drain and dry the quails. Cut along the backbone and press out flat.
For each quail, use your fingers to lift the skin off the breast. Push half a
slice of pancetta and two sage leaves under the skin of each bird. Season
quails with salt and pepper and brush generously with oil.

Cook quails on a medium-hot barbecue grill, turning once or twice, for
about 8 minutes or until crisped on the surface but breast meat is still
pink. Remove and let rest for a few minutes, before cutting each quail
into four pieces.

Spread endive and lettuce leaves over a large platter and arrange the
quails and artichokes on top.

In a small bowl, whisk the tapenade with the extra-virgin olive oil and spoon over the salad. Decorate the platter with lemon wedges.

 Grilled quail is easy to prepare for a crowd as it takes very little time to cook. As an alternative to the lettuce leaves, try a salad of finely sliced cucumber mixed with chopped spring onions or salad onion, and dressed with grain-mustard vinaigrette (page 243).

SERVES 8–12

Mushroom & spinach salad

250 g mixed oriental mushrooms (enokitake, oyster
and black fungus) or Swiss brown mushrooms

120 g small button mushrooms

juice and grated zest of ½ lime or 1 small lemon

¼ cup olive oil

1–2 cloves garlic, finely chopped

salt and freshly ground black pepper

120 g baby spinach leaves

60 g firm ricotta or Danish fetta cheese, crumbled
or cut into small cubes (optional)

Trim and slice Swiss and button mushrooms. Trim the ends from enokitake
mushrooms and separate. Shred oyster mushrooms and black fungus.
Place lime or lemon zest in a bowl with half the oil and set aside to infuse.

Heat remaining oil in a frying pan. Add garlic and fry for 20 seconds,
add the mushrooms and sauté over high heat until tender (2½–3 minutes).
Remove from the heat. Whisk lime or lemon juice into the flavoured oil,
and add salt and pepper. Pour dressing over the mushrooms and mix.

Spread the baby spinach leaves on a platter and cover with the mushrooms.
Garnish with the cheese, if using.

SERVES 3–4

Orangey beetroot salad

2 bunches baby beetroot

3 sprigs fresh thyme

50 g baby beetroot leaves or
   mixed small lettuce leaves

DRESSING

⅓ cup olive oil

juice and grated zest of
   ½ orange

2 teaspoons red wine vinegar

salt and freshly ground black
   pepper

2 anchovies, mashed (optional)

1 clove garlic, crushed

Trim the greens from the beetroot, leaving about 3 cm of the stems and 2 cm of the root. (By leaving some of the stem and the root on the beetroot it will bleed less of its colour into the cooking water.) Bring a pot of unsalted water to the boil and add the thyme and unpeeled beetroot. Boil until tender (about 25 minutes). (Alternatively, you can wrap the beetroots in foil and roast at 180°C for about 1 hour.) Tip into a colander and leave until cool enough to handle, then slip off the skins (wearing gloves to protect your hands from staining). Cut into quarters and put in a serving bowl.

To make the dressing, whisk together all ingredients. Spoon dressing over the beetroot and toss gently with the lettuce or baby beetroot leaves. Serve warm or allow to cool.

SERVES 4–6

Peppered Thai chicken salad

4 boneless chicken thighs,
   skin on

¼ cup vegetable oil, peanut oil
   or light olive oil

¼ cup fish sauce

2 teaspoons cracked black
   pepper

1½ tablespoons soft brown sugar
   or palm sugar

1 tablespoon white vinegar

1 teaspoon crushed garlic

½ cucumber, finely sliced

80 g bean sprouts

8-cm piece daikon (white
   radish) or yam bean, shredded

¾ cup finely shredded green
   pawpaw or under-ripe pear

1 large salad onion, finely sliced

2 large fresh mild red chillies or
   ½ red capsicum, deseeded and
   sliced

10 large fresh basil leaves,
   shredded

Place the chicken in a bowl with half the oil, half the fish sauce and
the black pepper. Set aside for 1 hour to marinate, turning occasionally.

In a large bowl, combine the remaining oil and fish sauce with the sugar,
vinegar and garlic. Add the cucumber, sprouts, daikon or yam bean,
pawpaw or pear, onion and chilli or capsicum. Toss until evenly coated
with the dressing. ➤

Heat a grill and when very hot grill the chicken, turning frequently, until the surface is crisp and the meat is cooked through (about 8 minutes). Set aside to rest for 5–6 minutes, then cut into thick slices.

Toss basil through the salad, then pile onto individual plates and arrange chicken slices on top.

SERVES 4

Prawn & cabbage noodle salad

1 × 50-g bundle dried thin egg
  noodles

1 onion, finely sliced

2 tablespoons vegetable oil

3 cloves garlic, finely chopped

1 small fresh red chilli, deseeded
  and chopped

6 thin slices fresh ginger,
  shredded

400–500 g wombok (Chinese
  cabbage), finely shredded

½ red capsicum, thinly sliced

80 g bean sprouts

soy and sesame dressing
  (page 239)

12–18 cooked prawns, peeled

sprigs of fresh coriander,
  for garnish

Cook the noodles in unsalted boiling water until tender (about 6 minutes), stirring to untangle the bundle.

In a wok, stir-fry the onion in the vegetable oil until tender. Add the garlic, chilli and ginger and cook briefly. Add the cabbage and capsicum and stir-fry over high heat until cabbage wilts and begins to soften (about 2 minutes). Add the bean sprouts and the soy and sesame dressing and stir for a few seconds. Remove from the heat.

Drain the noodles and add to the pan, along with the prawns. Mix well. Serve immediately, garnished with coriander.

SERVES 4

Roast duck & pumpkin salad

1 Chinese roast duck

½ jap or butternut pumpkin (about 600 g)

light olive oil

salt and freshly ground black pepper

100 g tatsoi and mizuna or other Asian leaves

5–6 sprigs fresh coriander

2 spring onions, finely sliced at an angle

1½ tablespoons toasted sesame seeds

¼ cup sweet chilli sauce

1 tablespoon light soy sauce

1 tablespoon rice vinegar

1 tablespoon water

2 teaspoons sugar

Preheat oven to 220°C. Wrap the duck in foil. Cut the pumpkin into 4-cm pieces. Place pumpkin in a baking tray lined with baking paper, sprinkle generously with oil, salt and pepper and stir to coat evenly. Place pumpkin in the oven, with the wrapped duck on a tray on another shelf. Bake pumpkin for 20–25 minutes, until tender. Remove and leave to cool. At this time, check the duck, which should be warmed through. If it is, remove from the oven, unwrap and remove the breasts and legs (reserving any juices). Cut the meat into chunks.

In a bowl, combine the duck and pumpkin with the tatsoi and mizuna leaves, sprigs of coriander and the spring onions (reserving some of the green tops for garnish).

To make the sweet chilli dressing, combine all the ingredients in a small bowl and stir until sugar has dissolved. Add the reserved duck juices to the dressing.

Pour dressing over the salad and mix lightly. Scatter with sesame seeds to serve.

Any leftover Chinese duck can be used to make a fabulous noodle soup.

SERVES 4–6

Roast vegetable salad with olives

1 sweet potato (about 250 g), cut into chunks

2 carrots, peeled and cut into chunks

3 kipfler potatoes, scrubbed and cut in half

2 zucchinis, cut into chunks

1–2 heads garlic, divided into cloves and tops trimmed

1 onion, cut into wedges

1 red capsicum, quartered and deseeded

extra-virgin olive oil

salt flakes and freshly ground black pepper

4–5 sprigs each of fresh rosemary and thyme

balsamic vinegar, classic aioli (page 233) or pesto (page 238), for dressing

24–30 black olives

a handful rocket or herbs, for garnish

Preheat oven to 190°C. Line two roasting pans with baking paper.

Place hard vegetables (sweet potato, carrots, kipflers) in one pan, and the softer vegetables (zucchini, garlic, onion, capsicum) in another. (Don't overcrowd the pans.) Drizzle vegetables generously with oil, sprinkle with salt and add the rosemary and thyme. Roast for 25–45 minutes, turning the vegetables several times during cooking. (Cooking time will depend on the size of the vegetable pieces, their hardness and the type of oven pan used. The tray of soft vegetables will be ready first.)

Combine all the vegetables in one of the pans. If dressing with balsamic vinegar, splash it generously into the hot pan and stir the vegetables around, adding plenty of freshly ground black pepper and a handful of black olives. If dressing with pesto or aioli, thin with a little extra olive oil before using if necessary, then transfer the vegetables to serving plates, scatter with olives and drizzle the dressing over. Garnish with the herbs or rocket leaves.

 Try other vegetables in this dish, such as celery hearts, bulb fennel, parsnip, pumpkin, eggplant and artichokes.

SERVES 6

Rosemary lamb & haloumi on herb salad

1 × 500-g lamb back strap

salt and freshly ground black pepper

2 tablespoons fruity olive oil

2 teaspoons finely chopped fresh rosemary

1 teaspoon finely chopped fresh thyme

1 large bunch watercress

4 sprigs flat-leaf parsley

8 sprigs fresh coriander

8 sprigs fresh chervil or tarragon

6–8 fresh basil leaves, torn

6–8 fresh mint leaves, torn

1 punnet spicy sprouts (onion, mustard and cress)

2 roma tomatoes, cut into thin wedges

½ small onion, cut into thin wedges

extra-virgin olive oil

3 teaspoons balsamic or red wine vinegar

250 g haloumi cheese, cut into 1-cm slices

Place the lamb in a shallow dish and season with salt and pepper. Drizzle with fruity olive oil and sprinkle on half the chopped herbs. Turn several times to coat with the oil and herbs, then set aside to marinate for at least 15 minutes.

Strip leaves from the watercress, parsley, coriander, and chervil or tarragon. Combine these in a bowl with the basil, mint, sprouts, tomatoes and onion. Drizzle with extra-virgin olive oil and vinegar. Season lightly. ❯

Heat a heavy pan or barbecue grill, brush with oil and cook the lamb, turning occasionally, until crisp on the surface but still pink inside (about 6 minutes). Set aside to rest for a few minutes, then slice.

Heat another pan and cook the sliced haloumi with 1½ tablespoons extra-virgin olive oil and the remaining chopped herbs, until the cheese is golden brown.

Place a small mound of herb salad on each serving plate and arrange lamb and haloumi slices on top. Top with more of the salad.

SERVES 4–6

Spice-crusted steak with cucumber salad

500–600 g beef rump or sirloin steaks (or use lamb or pork leg steaks, or lamb backstrap)

2 cloves garlic, crushed

olive oil

¾ teaspoon salt flakes

¾ teaspoon black peppercorns

1 tablespoon coriander seeds

2 teaspoons cumin seeds

½ teaspoon fennel seeds

2 onions, finely sliced

4 tomatoes, cut into thin wedges

1 Lebanese cucumber or ½ continental cucumber, finely sliced

1 fresh green chilli, deseeded and sliced

2–3 sprigs fresh coriander, leaves chopped

1 teaspoon salt

2 teaspoons sugar

¼ cup white vinegar

¾ cup natural yoghurt

lemon wedges, for garnish

Pat the steaks dry, rub with crushed garlic and brush with olive oil.

Coarsely grind the salt flakes, peppercorns and seeds in a mortar or spice grinder. Press mixture onto the steaks and set aside for 15 minutes.

In a bowl, combine the onion, tomatoes, cucumber, chilli and coriander. Season with 1 teaspoon salt and 2 teaspoons sugar and add the vinegar. Mix and leave to marinate. ➤

Heat a grill, barbecue or heavy pan to medium-high. Cook the steaks, turning once, until the surface is crisp and the inside pink (6–8 minutes). Remove from the heat and rest for 5 minutes, then slice thinly.

Drain liquid from the salad, pile onto individual plates and arrange the sliced meat on top. Add a dollop of yoghurt and garnish with a lemon wedge.

SERVES 4–6

Wilted lettuce salad with bacon

2 large slices fat bacon

1 clove garlic, finely chopped (optional)

1 tablespoon olive oil

1 mignonette or oak leaf lettuce

2 tablespoons grated parmesan, pecorino
  or other hard cheese

salt and freshly ground black pepper

balsamic, sherry or wine vinegar

Trim rind from bacon, and cut into small strips. Heat a large non-stick pan and fry the bacon, without oil, until almost crisp. Add the garlic, and a tablespoon of oil if the bacon has not provided much fat. Cook briefly, then remove from the heat.

Add the lettuce leaves to the hot pan and toss quickly so that they barely warm. Add the cheese, salt and pepper and a splash of vinegar.

Transfer immediately to a serving dish or pile onto individual plates. Serve at once.

SERVES 2–3

Wilted spinach with currants & pine nuts

1 bunch English spinach or 120 g spinach leaves

¼ cup extra-virgin olive oil

¼ cup pine nuts

¼ cup currants

salt and freshly ground black pepper

Remove tough stems from spinach leaves.

Heat a large non-stick pan and add the oil, pine nuts and currants. Stir over medium heat until the nuts are golden and the currants are round and plump (about 1½ minutes). Add the spinach and stir quickly to coat with the oil, but not to cook. Season with salt and pepper and transfer immediately to plates or a serving dish.

SERVES 2–3

Salads with beans, grains & pasta

The crunchy chewiness of grain-based salads makes them wholesome and satisfying meals in a bowl. Presented creatively they can also be interesting and appetising first courses.

Dried beans and lentils, cracked wheat and couscous, rice, pasta, noodles and bread are perfect foils for vibrant seasonings and dressings, and boldly flavoured ingredients like chorizo, olives and anchovies. For something different, try experimenting with renaissance grains like spelt, barley and quinoa.

< Bean sprout & cabbage salad with
coconut & crisp noodles (page 172)

Bean sprout & cabbage salad with coconut & crisp noodles

3 cups bean sprouts

150 g finely shredded wombok (Chinese cabbage)

1 salad onion, finely sliced

3 tablespoons chopped fresh coriander or basil

3–4 tablespoons flaked coconut

1–2 teaspoons grated fresh ginger

½ fresh hot red chilli, deseeded and finely shredded

50 g crisp noodles

DRESSING

1 tablespoon rice vinegar

¼ cup peanut oil

2 teaspoons clear honey

1 teaspoon crushed garlic

salt

Blanch sprouts in boiling water for 20 seconds, then drain and refresh in iced water. Drain again and combine with the cabbage, onion, herbs, coconut, ginger and chilli.

Make the dressing by whisking together all the ingredients.

Toss the salad with the dressing. Just before serving, stir in the crisp noodles.

 Bean sprouts look particularly elegant when their seedpods and tapering roots are plucked off. The Chinese call them 'silver sprouts'.

SERVES 3–5

Broad bean & spinach salad

400 g shelled broad beans, fresh or frozen

100 g baby spinach leaves

⅓ cup extra-virgin olive oil

2 tablespoons fresh lemon juice

50 g parmesan, pecorino or pepato cheese,
  shaved

freshly ground black pepper

Bring a large pot of lightly salted water to the boil and cook the broad beans for about 4 minutes, then drain and set aside to cool. Once cool, remove the outer pod by popping it off between your finger and thumb.

Combine the broad beans with the spinach and pile onto plates or into shallow bowls.

Whisk the oil and lemon juice together and drizzle over the salads, then scatter with the shaved cheese and season with plenty of pepper.

 Cooked broad beans look fantastic and taste twice as good when their wrinkly outer skins are removed to reveal the jade-green centres. It's worth the effort.

SERVES 4–5

Brown-rice salad with caramelised onion & grilled chorizo

1½ cups brown rice

2 large onions, sliced

1 red capsicum, thinly sliced

¼ cup olive oil

2 tablespoons balsamic vinegar

1 chorizo sausage, sliced

3 spring onions (white parts and 4 cm of greens), sliced

1 large clove garlic, chopped

3 tablespoons finely chopped fresh herbs, including some celery tops

¾ cup vinaigrette (page 243)

Boil the rice in a large pot of lightly salted water for about 35 minutes, until tender. Tip into a colander to drain and cool.

Meanwhile, sauté the onion and red capsicum in the olive oil for about 20 minutes, stirring frequently, until the onions are browned and caramelised and the capsicum is very tender. Add the balsamic vinegar and stir over medium heat until it evaporates. Tip onto a plate to cool.

Grill the chorizo in a non-stick pan until crisp, then remove and lightly fry the spring onions and garlic in the chorizo oil.

When all the cooked ingredients are cool, stir them through the rice, then mix in the fresh herbs and dressing.

SERVES 4–6

Cannellini bean salad
with bacon & onion

1½ cups dried cannellini (fagioli) beans

2-cm slice of smoked fat bacon (or use 2 bacon rashers)

1 onion, cut into quarters

3 cloves garlic, peeled

2 sprigs fresh thyme

olive oil

salt and freshly ground black pepper

1½ tablespoons fresh lemon juice

3 tablespoons chopped fresh parsley

Place the dried beans in a bowl and cover with plenty of cold water. Soak for about 12 hours, or overnight. Drain beans and transfer to a saucepan.

Trim rind from the bacon and add it to the saucepan, along with half the onion, two cloves of garlic and the thyme. Do not add salt, as it makes the beans tough. Cover generously with cold water and bring to the boil, then reduce to a simmer and cook for about 40 minutes, or until beans are tender.

Dice the bacon and remaining onion and sauté in 1 tablespoon oil, stirring frequently, until the onion is soft and lightly coloured and the bacon slightly crisp (about 5 minutes).

Drain the cooked beans and transfer to a shallow bowl. Add the bacon and onion, then stir in ¼ cup olive oil, adding salt and pepper to taste. Leave to cool.

When cool, add a little extra oil if necessary, plus the lemon juice and parsley and stir.

SERVES 4

 You can use two 400-g cans of cannellini beans instead of the dried beans. Or try vacuum-packed cooked beans, available from some supermarkets and specialty delicatessens. Just rinse and drain the beans, then mix with the cooked bacon and onions, add ⅓ cup olive oil, the lemon juice, parsley and seasonings to taste.

Cattivo salted ricotta & broccolini orecchiette salad

350 g broccolini florets

350 g dried orecchiette pasta

2 tablespoons olive oil

1 clove garlic, peeled

2 tablespoons salted capers, rinsed

2 tablespoons pinenuts, lightly toasted

sea salt and freshly ground black pepper

50 g salted ricotta cheese, coarsely grated

extra-virgin olive oil, to serve

Cook the broccolini in salted boiling water for 2 minutes, then drain and refresh in cold water. Drain again, then place on paper towels to drain completely.

Cook the pasta in a large saucepan of salted boiling water until al dente.

Meanwhile, heat oil in a frying pan. Add the garlic clove and fry until lightly browned. Remove garlic clove and discard. Add broccolini, capers, and pinenuts to the oil and toss over the heat for 1 minute. Remove from heat and season with salt and pepper.

Drain the cooked pasta and tip into a large bowl. Add the broccolini mixture and toss. Leave to cool for 4–5 minutes, to let the flavours infuse. **>**

Once cool, divide the salad into individual bowls, sprinkle salted ricotta over, and drizzle with some extra-virgin olive oil. Serve immediately.

Orecchiette (meaning 'little ears') is a type of durum-wheat pasta originating from Italy's Apulia (*Puglia*) region. In Italy, it is used mainly for festive occasions. It is available from any Italian deli, and many supermarkets.

SERVES 4

Chickpea potato salad

3 large potatoes (about 600 g)

1½ teaspoons ground turmeric

salt

1 × 420-g can chickpeas, rinsed
  and drained

1 onion, finely chopped

½ cup chopped fresh coriander

½ cup chopped fresh mint

1 cup natural yoghurt

1 teaspoon amchur (dried green
  mango powder) or 2 teaspoons
  fresh lemon juice

1 fresh hot green chilli,
  deseeded and finely chopped

2 teaspoons mild curry powder

8–10 cherry tomatoes, halved

Cut unpeeled potatoes into 2.5-cm cubes. Bring a saucepan of water to
the boil and add turmeric and 1 teaspoon salt. Boil potatoes until tender
(7–9 minutes), then tip into a colander and rinse under running cold water.
Leave to drain and cool.

In a salad bowl, combine the chickpeas, onion and most of the herbs with
the yoghurt, amchur or lemon juice, chilli and curry powder. Mix gently.

Stir the cooled potatoes into the salad, scatter with the cherry tomatoes
and garnish with remaining herbs.

SERVES 4–6

Couscous salad with orange & dates

1½ cups instant couscous

1½ cups boiling water

grated zest and juice of 1 lemon

2–3 tablespoons olive oil

salt and freshly ground black pepper

1 orange

⅔ cup chopped dates

¾ cup chopped fresh herbs (mint, basil, parsley)

Pour the couscous into a heatproof dish and add the boiling water and lemon juice. Stir and cover tightly with a plate or cling wrap and set aside for 10 minutes. (The grains will soften and expand, absorbing all of the liquid.) With a fork, fluff up the couscous and add the olive oil, salt and pepper. Leave to cool.

Grate the zest from the orange, then peel it. Working over a bowl to save the juices, remove the orange segments by cutting along either side of each segment, between the skin and the flesh.

Stir the lemon and orange zest into the couscous, along with the orange segments, dates and herbs.

SERVES 6

Curried rice salad
with prawns & mango

2 cups long-grain white rice

2 teaspoons curry powder

1½ teaspoons ground turmeric

salt

¾ cup mayonnaise (page 237)

2 tablespoons light olive oil
or water

1–2 tablespoons sweet chilli
sauce

freshly ground black pepper

120–180 g small peeled prawns

4 spring onions or 1 onion,
chopped

½ red capsicum, finely diced

½ stalk celery, finely sliced

¾ cup diced mango

3–4 tablespoons chopped fresh
herbs (mint, Vietnamese
mint, basil, coriander)

Cook the rice in a saucepan of well-salted boiling water for 10–12 minutes, until tender. Drain, rinse under running cold water to remove excess starch, drain again and tip into a bowl. While the rice is still warm, stir through the curry powder, turmeric and salt to taste. Leave to cool.

In a small bowl, whisk together the mayonnaise, oil or water, sweet chilli sauce and plenty of black pepper. Stir sauce through the rice, adding more salt if needed. Stir in the prawns, spring onions or onion, capsicum, celery, and most of the mango and herbs. Transfer to a serving dish and garnish with remaining mango and herbs.

SERVES 6–8

Italian tuna & white bean salad

1 × 450-g can tuna in oil, drained

2 × 400-g cans cannellini (fagioli) beans,
  rinsed and drained

1 salad onion, finely chopped

4–5 tablespoons extra-virgin olive oil

fresh lemon juice

salt and freshly ground black pepper

chopped fresh basil or parsley, for garnish

12 small black olives or stuffed green olives

2–3 hard-boiled eggs (see note on page 69),
  quartered (optional)

4–5 anchovies in oil, chopped (optional)

Flake the tuna into chunks and gently mix with the beans, onion and olive oil. Add lemon juice, salt and pepper to taste.

Transfer salad to a serving bowl or platter and garnish with herbs, olives, egg and anchovies (if using).

 Bacalao (dried salt cod), prepared and poached, can be substituted for the tuna.

SERVES 4–6

Mediterranean bread salad

½ loaf ciabatta, crusts removed and torn into pieces

extra-virgin olive oil

2 cloves garlic, peeled

1 loosely packed cup fresh basil leaves

4–6 well-ripened roma or hydroponic tomatoes

2–3 teaspoons white wine vinegar

salt and freshly ground black pepper

120 g rocket

24–30 small black kalamata or niçoise olives

Preheat oven to 200°C. Spread the bread on a baking tray and drizzle generously with oil. Bake for about 10 minutes, until crisp.

To make the dressing, crush the garlic and basil in a mortar. Cut tomatoes in half and squeeze juice into the mortar, then add 2½ tablespoons oil, the vinegar and seasoning to taste. Mix well.

Roughly chop the tomato flesh. Combine tomato, bread and rocket leaves in a bowl, add the dressing and toss.

Pile salad onto plates or into bowls and scatter the black olives on top.

SERVES 4–6

Mixed bean & celery salad

1½ cups mixed dried beans (borlotti, cannellini, kidney)
200 g green beans, cut into 4-cm lengths
1½ stalks celery, thinly sliced
1 cup chopped celery leaves
1 salad onion, finely chopped
¾–1 teaspoon celery salt or salt flakes
freshly ground black pepper
⅔ cup grain-mustard vinaigrette (page 243)

Place dried beans in a bowl, cover with plenty of cold water and soak overnight. Drain, then transfer to a large saucepan, cover with fresh unsalted water and bring to the boil. Reduce heat and simmer for about 45 minutes, until tender. Tip into a colander to drain and cool.

Boil the green beans in lightly salted water for about 3 minutes, until tender but still a little bit crisp. Drain, refresh in cold water and drain again.

Transfer cooled mixed beans to a bowl and add the green beans, celery, celery leaves and onion. Stir in salt and black pepper and the dressing.

Leave for at least 20 minutes before serving.

SERVES 4–6

Pasta salad with roast chicken & rocket pesto

250–300 g pasta (spirals, penne, bows or macaroni)
½ cup rocket pesto (page 238)
3 tablespoons olive oil, mayonnaise or sour cream
1½ cups diced roast chicken
4 spring onions (white parts and 12 cm of greens), chopped
50 g sun-dried or semi-dried tomatoes, chopped
50 g baby spinach leaves
freshly ground black pepper

Cook pasta in a large saucepan of salted boiling water until al dente (10–12 minutes). Drain well and transfer to a mixing bowl. Add the pesto and oil (if using) to the pasta and leave for about 10 minutes to cool. (Do not add mayonnaise or sour cream at this point.)

When the pasta is cool, stir in the chicken, spring onions, tomatoes and spinach, and the mayonnaise or sour cream (if using) and mix well. Add salt and pepper to taste.

Transfer to a salad bowl or serve in individual shallow bowls.

SERVES 4

Penne with capsicum, olives & anchovies

300 g penne pasta

¾ cup grain-mustard vinaigrette (page 243)

¾ cup peas or sliced green beans

1 cup diced capsicum (a mixture of red, yellow and green)

½ cup diced salad onion

½ cup diced cucumber

½ cup diced cheese (fetta, haloumi, cheddar or firm goat's cheese)

¼ cup sliced kalamata olives

4 anchovy fillets, chopped

2–3 tablespoons finely chopped fresh parsley, mint or basil

Bring a saucepan of salted water to the boil and cook the penne for 10–12 minutes, until al dente. Drain, then tip into a bowl. Add two-thirds of the dressing and set aside to cool.

Boil the peas or beans in lightly salted water until barely cooked, then drain. Add to the pasta.

In another bowl, combine the capsicum, onion, cucumber, cheese, olives and anchovies. Add remaining dressing, toss, and set aside.

When pasta is completely cool, stir in the diced vegetable mixture and the herbs.

SERVES 3–6

Turkish lentil salad

1½ cups dried lentils

3–4 tablespoons olive oil

2 tablespoons fresh lemon juice

salt and freshly ground black pepper

2 large vine-ripened tomatoes, deseeded and chopped

1 small salad onion, finely chopped

1 clove garlic, finely chopped

2 tablespoons chopped fresh mint or basil

2 tablespoons chopped fresh parsley

8–10 kalamata olives

1½ tablespoons drained capers

2 tablespoons Persian or Danish fetta cheese, diced

Rinse the lentils, then boil in unsalted water until tender (15–50 minutes depending on the lentils used.) Drain and tip into a large bowl. Add half the olive oil and lemon juice, plus salt and pepper to taste. Stir and leave to cool.

Combine remaining olive oil and lemon juice with the tomato, onion, garlic, herbs, and salt and pepper. Add to the lentils and stir.

Transfer to a serving dish and garnish with olives, capers and fetta.

 French puy lentils are best for salads. Try them served very simply with a vinaigrette and some sliced salad onion.

SERVES 4–5

Vietnamese rice-noodle salad with lime & peanut dressing

60–70 g rice vermicelli

2 snake beans or 6 green beans, sliced

2 Lebanese cucumbers or 1 small continental cucumber, deseeded and thinly sliced

½ red capsicum or 2 large fresh red chillies, shredded

1½ cups bean sprouts, blanched and refreshed

1 spring onion, finely sliced at an angle

1 small bunch fresh coriander, separated into sprigs

1 small bunch fresh basil, separated into leaves and small sprigs

lime and peanut dressing (page 234)

lettuce leaves, to serve

Soak the rice vermicelli in boiling water until softened, then drain well.

Cook the beans in lightly salted water for about 2½ minutes, until tender but still a little crisp. Drain, then refresh in cold water and drain again.

In a large bowl, combine the cucumber, capsicum or chilli, bean sprouts, beans, spring onion and herbs. Drizzle the lime-peanut dressing over the salad and stir well.

Arrange lettuce leaves in bowls or on a platter, spread the rice vermicelli over the leaves, and spoon on the salad mix.

SERVES 4–6

Classics

Every cuisine has its signature recipes, many of them salads. In America it's the hundred-year-old Waldorf salad of Waldorf Astoria Hotel fame, along with the Caesar, named for its creator Caesar Cardini and first popular with the 1920s Hollywood set.

In Greece the favourite salad is simplicity at its best: fresh-from-the-vine tomatoes and cucumber, offset by salty kalamata olives and firm white cheese, glistening with oil and studded with herbs.

Niçoise vies with celeriac remoulade as France's best classic salad, while coleslaw and potato salad are perennial favourites worldwide.

Why do certain dishes become classics? Probably because they taste great!

‹ Caesar salad (page 198)

Caesar salad

3 large cloves garlic, crushed

extra-virgin olive oil

2–3 thick slices day-old bread

2 heads cos lettuce
  or 4–6 little gem cos lettuce

70 g anchovy fillets in oil,
  drained

1 whole egg, plus 1 yolk

1 tablespoon Dijon mustard

3 teaspoons white wine
  or cider vinegar

⅔ cup vegetable oil

100 g parmesan

freshly ground black pepper

Preheat oven to 180°C. Mix two-thirds of the garlic with ¼ cup olive oil and brush over the bread. Cut bread into 3-cm chunks and spread on an oven tray. Bake for about 15 minutes, turning several times, until golden-brown.

Tear lettuce leaves into pieces and place in a large bowl. Chop two or three anchovy fillets and cut the remainder in half lengthways.

To make the dressing, whisk the egg and yolk with the mustard, vinegar and remaining garlic. Slowly whisk in the vegetable oil and ⅓ cup olive oil to make a thin, creamy sauce. Grate half the parmesan and stir into the sauce along with the chopped anchovies. Shave the remaining parmesan. Toss the anchovy strips, shaved parmesan and croutons through the lettuce, add the dressing and toss lightly. Season generously with black pepper.

SERVES 4

Celeriac remoulade

1 celeriac (about 500 g), peeled

fresh lemon juice

salt

3–4 tablespoons chopped fresh
  herbs (parsley, tarragon,
  chervil, basil)

1 cup mayonnaise (page 237)

1–2 anchovy fillets, chopped

1½ tablespoons capers, chopped

2 teaspoons Dijon mustard

freshly ground black pepper

snow pea sprouts or chives,
  for garnish

Cut celeriac into chunks and pass through the shredder attachment of a food processor (or use a sharp knife to cut into fine sticks.) Place in a bowl, add a squeeze of lemon juice and a large pinch of salt and cover with cold water. Set aside.

Stir the herbs into the mayonnaise, along with the anchovies, capers, mustard and salt and pepper.

Drain the celeriac and dry in a clean tea towel.

Stir the dressing through the celeriac and garnish with snow pea sprouts or chives.

SERVES 3–4

Coleslaw

600–700 g white cabbage
1 large carrot, peeled and coarsely grated
1 onion, finely sliced
1½ cups coleslaw dressing (page 237)
fresh lemon juice
handful chopped fresh parsley

Use a sharp knife or mandolin slicer to finely shred the cabbage. Separate the strands by combing your fingers through, then transfer to a large bowl. Add carrot and onion and mix well.

In a small bowl, whip the coleslaw dressing, adding lemon juice to taste and thinning with a little cold water.

Stir dressing through the salad, and add chopped parsley.

 Coleslaw is usually served at room temperature. Red cabbage and crinkly wombok (Chinese cabbage) can replace some of the white cabbage if desired. You can also add capsicum that has been cut into fine strips.

SERVES 4–6

Egg salad

10 hard-boiled eggs (see note on page 69)

2 tablespoons finely chopped red onion

2 spring onions, finely chopped

1½ tablespoons finely chopped fresh dill

1½ tablespoons finely chopped fresh parsley

3 tablespoons sour cream

2 tablespoons mayonnaise (page 237)

½ clove garlic crushed with ¾ teaspoon salt

white pepper

Shell the cooled hard-boiled eggs and chop roughly. Place in a bowl and mix with the onions and herbs.

Mix the sour cream and mayonnaise with the garlic and pepper, then gently stir through the salad. Set aside for a few minutes before serving.

SERVES 4–8

Greek salad

4–6 vine-ripened tomatoes

1½ Lebanese cucumbers or 1 large continental cucumber

1 red or white onion, thinly sliced

24 small kalamata olives

200 g Greek fetta or firm sheep's milk cheese

2–3 sprigs fresh thyme

1–2 sprigs fresh oregano

extra-virgin olive oil

salt flakes

Cut the tomatoes into thick slices or wedges and cut the cucumber into chunks.

Arrange the tomato, cucumber and onion on plates or a serving platter. Scatter the olives over and add the cheese (either in a single piece or cut into cubes).

Strip leaves from thyme and oregano sprigs and chop. Scatter herbs over the salad, drizzle generously with olive oil and season with salt.

SERVES 4

Insalata Caprese

1 bunch fresh basil
10–12 pieces bocconcini
6–9 small vine-ripened tomatoes
salt flakes
freshly ground black pepper
extra-virgin olive oil

Strip basil leaves from stems. Cut each piece of bocconcini into three slices. Thickly slice the tomatoes.

Arrange the tomato slices side by side on a large platter and season lightly with salt. Place a basil leaf on each tomato slice, then top with a slice of bocconcini. Finish with plenty of freshly ground black pepper and a generous drizzle of olive oil.

SERVES 4–8

Potato salad

½ cup boiling chicken stock

1 white onion, finely chopped

2½ tablespoons cider or white vinegar

6 waxy potatoes (about 1 kg)

¼ cup light olive oil or salad oil

⅔ cup sour cream

2 teaspoons grainy mustard

salt and freshly ground black pepper

chopped fresh parsley or chives, for garnish

Combine the chicken stock and onion in a bowl with the vinegar. Place unpeeled potatoes in a saucepan of lightly salted water, cover and bring to the boil. Reduce heat and simmer until potatoes are tender (about 15 minutes). Drain, and while still hot carefully peel off the skins. Cut into chunks and put into a large bowl. Pour on the vinegar mixture, cover and set aside to allow potatoes to absorb the liquid.

Stir oil, sour cream and mustard together, adding salt and pepper to taste. Stir this dressing into the potato mix, then transfer to a serving dish. Garnish with chopped parsley or chives.

 Waxy potatoes are best for salads as they hold their shape and don't break up. Try nicola, patrone, pink fir apple and yellow-fleshed kipfler varieties.

SERVES 4–6

Russian salad

1 large potato, diced

1 carrot, peeled and diced

¾ cup peas

1 × 450-g can baby beetroot (or use cooked fresh beetroot)

1 green apple, diced

2 tablespoons mayonnaise (page 237)

2 tablespoons sour cream

chopped fresh parsley or dill

salt and black or white pepper

Bring two small saucepans of water to the boil and salt generously. Boil the potato in one pan and the carrot in the other. When carrot is almost cooked, add the peas and cook until tender. Drain and refresh carrot and peas in cold water, then drain again. Drain potatoes when tender and transfer to a plate to cool.

Drain the beetroot, rinse in cold water, then dice finely.

Combine the potato, carrot, peas, apple and beetroot in a serving bowl. Stir in the mayonnaise, sour cream and herbs, and season to taste with salt and pepper.

SERVES 4

Salade Niçoise

200 g green beans, cut in half

2–3 stalks celery, finely sliced

1 cucumber, thickly sliced

4 firm ripe tomatoes, cut into wedges

1 small salad onion, cut into thin wedges

2 spring onions (white parts and 6 cm of greens), sliced

9–12 anchovy fillets, halved lengthways

18–24 small black olives

12 small fresh basil leaves (optional)

1 clove garlic, very finely chopped (optional)

salt

extra-virgin olive oil

6 hard-boiled eggs (see note on page 69), cut into quarters

Blanch beans for 3–5 minutes in lightly salted water, until bright green and tender but still a little crisp. Drain and refresh in iced water, then drain again.

In a serving bowl, combine the beans, celery, cucumber, tomatoes, onions, anchovies, olives and basil (if using). Sprinkle on chopped garlic (if using), season with salt and drizzle with olive oil. Arrange egg pieces on top.

 Vegetables such as baby artichokes, baby carrots and broad beans can also be used in this salad. Canned tuna is another common addition.

SERVES 6

Tabbouleh

1 cup burghul (cracked wheat)

4 roma tomatoes

3 cups flat-leaf parsley

1½ cups fresh mint leaves

½ cup chopped onion

juice of 1 large lemon

½ cup fruity light olive oil

1 large clove garlic, crushed (optional)

salt and freshly ground black pepper

Tip the burghul into a heatproof dish and cover with warm water. Set aside for about half an hour, to allow grains to soften and expand slightly. Tip into a colander to drain and leave for about 5 minutes.

Cut the tomatoes in half and scoop the seeds and pulpy inner flesh into a sieve over a bowl (reserve the juice). Finely dice the firm flesh. Finely chop the parsley, including some stems, and finely chop the mint leaves.

In a large bowl, combine the diced tomato, onion, parsley and mint.

To make the dressing, add the lemon juice to the reserved tomato juice, along with the olive oil and garlic (if using). Whisk well.

Stir the cracked wheat into the tomato and herb mixture, then add the dressing, and salt and pepper to taste. Mix well.

SERVES 4–6

Waldorf salad

1 green apple, cored and cut into chunks

2 red apples, cored and cut into chunks

2 stalks celery, sliced

¾ cup mayonnaise (page 237) or a mixture
of mayonnaise and sour cream

½ cup pecan or walnut halves

In a mixing bowl combine the apple, celery and mayonnaise, then stir in the nuts.

Try a new twist on this classic by substituting bulb fennel, nashi pears or other crisp Asian pears, or sliced star fruit (carambola) for some of the apple.

SERVES 4–5

Fruity salads

Fruit salads are just the thing for fresh, crisp and tangy desserts that taste fabulous. But they are also wonderful served ice-cold in chilled glasses or bowls as palate-stimulating first courses, or teamed with platters of cold cuts and grilled meats on a party buffet table. As side-dishes they marry superbly with rich meats like pork and duck.

Check out Asian groceries for interesting fruits like citrusy pomelos, sweet and juicy lychees and longans, elegant star-shaped carambolas, and tart unripe mangoes and papayas.

< Duck & kiwifruit salad (page 216)

Duck & kiwifruit salad

300–400 g boneless honey-roasted duck or Peking roast duck

4–5 kiwifruit

watercress, curly endive or little gem cos lettuce

¼ cup slivered almonds, toasted

1 tablespoon raspberry vinegar

2 tablespoons light olive oil

salt and freshly ground black pepper

Cut the duck into strips or bite-sized cubes. Peel the kiwifruit and cut into wedges.

Combine duck, kiwifruit, greens and almonds in a serving bowl. Drizzle on vinegar and oil and season to taste. Toss gently.

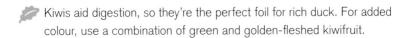 Kiwis aid digestion, so they're the perfect foil for rich duck. For added colour, use a combination of green and golden-fleshed kiwifruit.

SERVES 4

Exotic fruit salad

½ red papaya, cubed

1 mango, cubed

2 bananas, thickly sliced

2 carambolas (star fruit), thinly sliced

2 thick slices sweet pineapple, rind on, cut into wedges

1 × 440-g can jackfruit, lychees or other Asian fruit, drained

SYRUP

½ cup white sugar or pale palm sugar

2 star anise

½ teaspoon green peppercorns

2 strips lime zest

1 cup water

Make a flavoured syrup by combining the sugar, star anise, peppercorns and lime zest in 1 cup water and simmering for 5 minutes, until sugar dissolves. Remove from heat and let stand for at least 30 minutes, to allow flavours to develop.

Combine all the fruit in a serving bowl and pour the syrup over. Cover and chill for at least 30 minutes before serving.

SERVES 6

Festive melon salad

½ rockmelon

½ honeydew melon

1 wedge champagne watermelon
(optional)

1 wedge pink watermelon

1 mango

1 × 440-g can lychees

lychee liqueur

juice of 1–2 fresh limes

5–6 star anise or 2 split vanilla
beans (optional)

fresh mint sprigs, for garnish

Peel the rockmelon and honeydew melon and scoop out the seeds with
a spoon. Cut into large, thin slices or chunks. Trim the skin and white rind
from the watermelon wedges and cut flesh into slivers or chunks. Peel the
mango and cut the flesh into slivers or chunks. Drain the lychees, reserving
their liquid.

In a large bowl, combine the melon, mango and lychees. Flavour the reserved
lychee liquid with liqueur and lime juice to taste, and add the star anise or
vanilla beans (if using). Pour liquid over the salad, cover and chill for at least
20 minutes. Garnish with mint before serving.

SERVES 6–8

Fig, orange & prosciutto salad

6 figs

2 oranges, peeled

6 slices prosciutto

120 g wild rocket

1 tablespoon raspberry vinegar or red wine vinegar

¼ cup light olive oil

1 teaspoon clear honey

½ teaspoon chopped fresh red chilli

shaved parmesan, to serve

Cut the figs into thick slices. Working over a bowl to save the juices, remove the orange segments by cutting along either side of each segment, between the skin and the flesh.

Preheat grill to hot. Place prosciutto on an oven tray and grill until crisp. Set aside to cool. Spread rocket leaves over a serving platter and scatter on the orange segments. Arrange the sliced figs on top.

Whisk together the vinegar, 1 tablespoon of reserved orange juice, the olive oil, honey and chilli and drizzle over the salad. Crumble the prosciutto over the salad and garnish with some shaved parmesan.

SERVES 4–6

Mango & avocado salad
with smoked chicken

1 small bunch watercress or ½ punnet snow pea sprouts

2 large mangos, cut into chunks

2 avocados, cut into chunks

2 smoked chicken breasts (about 350 g), cut into chunks

2 tablespoons finely shredded fresh mint or basil leaves

1–2 tablespoons fresh lime or lemon juice

1½ teaspoons grainy mustard (optional)

salt and freshly ground black pepper

½ cup roasted cashew nuts

Separate the watercress into small sprigs, or trim the ends off the snow pea sprouts.

In a salad bowl, combine the mango, avocado, chicken, watercress or sprouts, and herbs.

Mix lime or lemon juice with mustard (if using), and season with salt and pepper. Carefully fold dressing through the salad and scatter on the nuts. Chill before serving.

SERVES 4–6

Moroccan orange, onion & black olive salad

3–4 large oranges

1 small red onion, sliced into rings

12–18 black manzanilla olives
   or other small black olives, rinsed

DRESSING

2 tablespoons fresh lemon juice

½ teaspoon ground cumin

⅓ teaspoon harissa or other hot chilli paste

salt

Peel the oranges, removing all white pith. Slice thickly and arrange on a platter with the slices overlapping. Scatter onion rings and olives over the top.

To make the dressing, whisk the lemon juice with the cumin and harissa or chilli paste in a small bowl, and season with salt. Drizzle evenly over the salad. Cover and refrigerate for at least 20 minutes before serving.

SERVES 3–5

Pear & pancetta salad
with walnuts & blue cheese

2 firm ripe pears

2 teaspoons softened butter

1 teaspoon soft brown sugar

4 thin slices pancetta

½ small head curly endive
or coral lettuce

2 tablespoons chopped walnuts

2 tablespoons crumbled blue
cheese

2 tablespoons walnut oil

red wine vinegar

salt flakes and freshly ground
black pepper

Cut each pear in half (or quarters if you prefer) and remove the seed core
and woody stem. Combine butter and sugar and spread over the cut surface
of the pears. Place pears cut-side down in a hot pan and cook until the
surface is glazed and golden-brown. Remove and leave to cool, then crisp
the pancetta in the hot pan. Remove and drain on paper towels.

Spread greens on individual plates and scatter over the walnuts and cheese.
Arrange pear pieces on top of the salad. Drizzle with walnut oil and a little red
wine vinegar, and add a pinch of salt flakes and a big grind of black pepper.

 You could substitute crisp red apples, fennel or yam bean for the
pears – use them raw, and brush the cut surface of the apples or
yam bean with lemon juice to prevent discolouration.

SERVES 2

Som tam (Thai green papaya salad)

1 firm green (unripe) papaya, or 1 large green mango

1 carrot, peeled

1 small onion, peeled

1 clove garlic, peeled

2 teaspoons dried prawns

2–3 teaspoons roasted peanuts or cashew nuts

1 small fresh red chilli, deseeded

juice of 2 large limes

2½ tablespoons fish sauce

soft brown sugar or palm sugar

banana leaf, lettuce leaves or wombok (Chinese cabbage) leaves, to serve

Using a vegetable peeler or fine grater, shred the papaya or mango and carrot, and very finely shred or grate the onion. Mix these together in a bowl.

Grind the garlic, prawns, nuts and chilli to a paste in a mortar or spice grinder. Add the lime juice, fish sauce and sugar to taste and mix well.

Pour the dressing over the salad and leave for at least 20 minutes before serving.

If you can obtain a piece of banana leaf, cut squares from it to line the serving plates, or alternatively present the som tam in lettuce cups or trimmed wombok leaves.

SERVES 4–6

Thai pink grapefruit salad

2 ruby grapefruits or 1 pomelo

2 spring onions (white parts and 15 cm of greens), chopped

1 bundle fresh enokitake mushrooms (or use a 4-cm piece dried wood-ear mushroom, soaked)

100 g bean sprouts, blanched and refreshed

80 g curly endive

12 sprigs fresh coriander

12 fresh mint leaves, shredded

12 large fresh sweet basil leaves, shredded

juice and zest of 1 lime

1½ tablespoons fish sauce

1–3 teaspoons palm sugar

1 large fresh mild red chilli, deseeded and shredded

With a sharp knife, peel the grapefruits, removing all skin and pith. Working over a bowl to save the juices, remove the segments by cutting along either side of each segment, between the skin and the flesh. Place segments into a bowl with the spring onions. Trim the root stub from the enokitake mushrooms to separate them. If using wood-ear mushroom, drain and shred finely. Add mushrooms, sprouts, curly endive and herbs to the grapefruit.

Stir lime juice and zest into the reserved grapefruit juice, and stir in the fish sauce and palm sugar. Add additional sugar or fish sauce if needed. Pour half the dressing over the salad, mix well and serve into small bowls. Drizzle with remaining dressing and garnish with chilli.

SERVES 3–4

Watermelon & onion salad with crumbled fetta

900 g watermelon

¾ cup fresh mint, basil or coriander leaves

1 white onion, finely sliced

juice of 1 lime

1 tablespoon fruity olive oil

1 teaspoon Dijon or grainy mustard

salt

80 g rocket

100 g fetta cheese or haloumi, crumbled or diced

Cube the watermelon, cutting on a large plate to catch the juices. (You should get about 6 cups cubed fruit.) Cut mint or basil leaves into strips.

Combine watermelon and onion in a serving bowl and toss lightly.

To make the dressing, whisk the lime juice, oil, mustard and salt into ¼ cup of the reserved watermelon juice. Drizzle over the salad.

Just before serving, stir in the herbs and rocket leaves and scatter with the cheese.

SERVES 6

Dressings & sauces

Rich and creamy, hot and spicy, tangy or mellow — salad dressings have myriad flavour possibilities. They give a salad its personality, its passion.

Pre-made salad dressings can be purchased, of course, but few compare with the zingy taste of a freshly whisked vinaigrette, a glossy homemade mayonnaise, or a zappy blend of Asian seasonings and sauces.

Dress leafy salads sparingly, and preferably just before taking to the table, so they don't become soggy. Cooked vegetables, meats and coleslaws generally benefit from a more generous dousing with dressing — take extra to the table if you like.

Good cooking encourages experimentation. Try adding your own touches to these tasty dressings and sauces.

‹ Chilli lime dressing (page 232)

Chilli lime dressing

3 tablespoons fresh lime juice

2 tablespoons fish sauce

1 tablespoon sweet chilli sauce

2–3 teaspoons palm sugar
   or soft brown sugar

Whisk all ingredients together in a bowl or shake in a screw top jar.

This dressing keeps for 2–3 weeks in the refrigerator.

MAKES ⅔ CUP

Classic aioli

1 egg yolk
1½ teaspoons Dijon mustard
⅓ teaspoon sea salt flakes
3–4 cloves garlic, crushed
½ cup light olive oil
¼ cup fruity olive oil

Whisk the egg yolk with the mustard, salt and garlic in a mixing bowl until creamy (or mix in a food processor). Whisk in light olive oil and fruity olive oil. If aioli is too thick, it can be thinned by whisking in 2–4 tablespoons cool water.

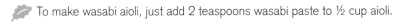 To make wasabi aioli, just add 2 teaspoons wasabi paste to ½ cup aioli.

MAKES 1½ CUPS

Lime & peanut dressing

⅓ cup fresh lime juice

1¼ tablespoons palm sugar or soft brown sugar

½ teaspoon salt

1–2 cloves garlic, crushed

2 tablespoons finely chopped roasted peanuts

In a small bowl, combine the lime juice, sugar and salt, stirring until sugar is dissolved. Add the garlic and peanuts. Leave for about 20 minutes before using.

 To make a spicy Vietnamese dressing, use a little less lime juice, omit the salt, and add ¼ cup fish sauce, ⅓ cup water and 1–2 teaspoons chopped fresh hot red chilli. (You can also substitute cucumber for the nuts if you like.)

MAKES ⅔ CUP

Mayonnaise

1 egg yolk
1½ teaspoons Dijon mustard
⅓ teaspoon sea salt flakes
¾–1 cup light olive oil
1 teaspoon fresh lemon juice

Whisk the egg yolk with the mustard and salt in a mixing bowl until creamy (or blend in a food processor). Add a few teaspoons of oil and whisk well to establish the emulsion – the mixture will begin to thicken and turn light in colour. Add the remaining oil in a thin stream, whisking energetically to incorporate it into the emulsion. The mayonnaise will become quite thick and a cream colour. When all the oil has been added, whisk in the lemon juice.

 To make lime mayonnaise, replace the mustard with the grated zest of 1 lime, and replace the lemon juice with lime juice. Or to make coleslaw dressing, add 2 tablespoons sour cream, 2 teaspoons clear honey and 1 tablespoon lemon juice to ¾ cup mayonnaise (makes 1 cup).

MAKES 1½ CUPS

Pesto

1 large bunch fresh basil

2–3 cloves garlic, peeled

2 tablespoons pine nuts

1–1⅓ cups freshly grated parmesan cheese

½ teaspoon sea salt flakes

⅔–¾ cup extra-virgin olive oil

Strip basil leaves from stems and tear large leaves in half. Place basil in a mortar or food processor with the garlic, pine nuts, parmesan and salt. Grind until well chopped, then scrape down the sides of the bowl. Blend while slowly adding enough oil to make a thick, bright-green sauce.

If keeping pesto for more than a few days, omit the parmesan during preparation and stir it in just before serving. Freshly made pesto can be refrigerated for up to 1 week. To keep for up to 2 weeks, transfer to a small glass dish or jar and smooth the top, then cover with a 1-cm layer of olive oil (pour the oil off before using).

 To make rocket pesto, just use small-leaf rocket leaves instead of basil.

MAKES 2 CUPS

Soy & sesame dressing

¼ cup sesame oil

1½ tablespoons light soy sauce

1 teaspoon castor sugar

1½ teaspoons tahini mixed with
   2 tablespoons cold water (optional)

In a small bowl, whisk together oil, soy and sugar until sugar has dissolved.

For a creamy dressing, add the tahini mixture and mix well.

This dressing keeps for 2–3 weeks in the refrigerator.

MAKES ⅓ CUP

Spicy nut sauce

1 onion, very finely chopped

2 cloves garlic, crushed

1 tablespoon vegetable oil

3 teaspoons ground coriander

½ teaspoon ground cumin

½ teaspoon chilli flakes or hot chilli paste

2 teaspoons palm sugar or soft brown sugar

1 teaspoon salt, or to taste

1¼ cups coconut cream

2–3 tablespoons peanut butter (or use macadamia or cashew butter)

1–2 teaspoons kecap manis (sweet soy sauce)

In a small saucepan, cook the onion and garlic in the oil until softened (about 2 minutes). Add the spices, chilli, sugar, salt and coconut cream. Bring to the boil, then reduce heat and simmer for about 3 minutes, stirring occasionally, until thickened. Stir in the nut butter and simmer for another minute, then season with the kecap manis and check for salt. Allow to cool before using.

This sauce keeps for about 1 week in the refrigerator.

MAKES 1½ CUPS

Tapenade

1 cup pitted black olives

50 g anchovies in oil, drained

3 tablespoons drained capers

2 tablespoons fresh lemon juice

freshly ground black pepper

¼ cup extra-virgin olive oil

Place all of the ingredients in a blender or food processor and grind to a thick paste.

Transfer to a small dish or jar and smooth the top. To keep the tapenade for more than 1 week, cover with at least 1 cm of olive oil (pour the oil off before using).

MAKES 1½ CUPS

Vinaigrette

¼ cup extra-virgin olive oil

1 tablespoon white or red wine vinegar

1 small clove garlic, finely chopped or crushed

1 teaspoon Dijon mustard (optional)

salt and freshly ground black pepper

Whisk all the ingredients together in a small bowl, or shake in a small screw-top jar.

Vinaigrette can be kept for a week or two in the refrigerator.

 To make a grain-mustard vinaigrette, just add 2–3 teaspoons grainy mustard.

MAKES ⅓ CUP

Special ingredients

AMCHOR is dried green mango that has been ground into a powder. It is used in Indian cooking for its tangy flavour. Lemon juice can be used instead.

BABY SPINACH LEAVES are English spinach leaves that have been picked young and can be eaten raw.

BALSAMIC VINEGAR is a dark, aged vinegar with a mellow flavour. Often used in salad dressings.

BANH TRANG are dry rice paper sheets used to make Vietnamese rice paper rolls. Soften for 30 seconds in warm water immediately before using.

BEAN THREAD NOODLES are translucent fine noodles made from mung beans. Soak in hot water to soften before use.

BUCKWHEAT NOODLES are Japanese noodles made from buckwheat flour. A favourite ingredient in cold salads.

BUTTER LETTUCE is a soft-leaf lettuce with a mild flavour, which is usually grown hydroponically. Handle with care to avoid bruising the leaves.

CHOKO is a pear-shaped, wrinkly vegetable (sometimes classified as a fruit) with a fairly bland taste and a crunchy texture.

CORAL LETTUCE is a small-head lettuce with pale-green or dark purple-red leaves. Very decorative and readily available for use in salad mixes.

COS LETTUCE is a long-leaf lettuce with thick stems and dark-green outer leaves. With a crisp texture, it is the lettuce used for Caesar salads.

CUMIN is a pungent spice used in Indian and Middle Eastern cooking. Sold as whole seeds or ground.

CURLY ENDIVE (also known as frisee) is a lettuce with frilly, lacy leaves. The outer leaves are dark-green and bitter, but the inner leaves are pale-green and mild. Very decorative, this lettuce is used in salad mixes and as a garnish. **Witlof** is a different kind of salad vegetable that is sometimes also called endive.

DAIKON is a giant white radish used in Japanese and Chinese cuisines. It has a mild, peppery flavour. It is sold in Asian groceries, or can be replaced with fresh red radish.

FENNEL SEEDS are seeds from the fennel herb, and have a distinctive anise-liquorice flavour. Used in many spice mixes, fennel seeds are excellent with seafood and tomatoes.

FETTA CHEESE is a firm salty cheese, traditionally made from sheep or goat's milk. It is sold packed in brine. **Haloumi** can replace it in most recipes.

HALOUMI is a firm salty cheese, traditionally made with a mixture of sheep and goat's milk. Packed in brine, this cheese is suitable for grilling or frying due to its high melting point.

ICEBERG LETTUCE is a round-head lettuce with tightly packed leaves. It is enjoyed for its mild flavour and crisp texture. Keep iceberg lettuce in a covered container in the refrigerator to maintain crispness. Whole leaves can be used as edible bowls/plates (as in the som tam recipe). Tear into chunks or shred to add to salads.

KECAP MANIS is a thick, sweetened soy sauce used in Indonesian cookery for its rich, deep colour and flavour.

LEMONGRASS is a stem-like herb with a woody texture and distinct citrus flavour. Only the lower 16 cm of the stem should be used, and it should always be ground or very finely chopped. It is used to flavour Asian-style dressings and is readily available where Asian foods and fresh herbs are sold. It can be refrigerated for several weeks.

LITTLE GEM COS LETTUCE is the miniature version of **cos lettuce**, with decorative small leaves.

MANCHEGO is a firm Spanish sheep's milk cheese that has a rich, smooth flavour.

MIGNONETTE is a small-head lettuce with green or purple-tinged leaves and a mild flavour. You can use butter, coral or cos lettuce instead.

MIZUNA is a mild-flavoured Asian soft-leaf herb that is often included in salad mixes but is also sold separately. It makes an attractive garnish.

PANCETTA is a spiced, dry-cured Italian ham. It is grilled or fried until crisp before being added to salads. Bacon or prosciutto can replace it.

PECORINO is an Italian sheep's milk cheese, usually sharp-flavoured with a hard texture. Substitute parmesan cheese if necessary.

PEPATO is a semi-hard Italian sheep's milk cheese with peppercorns.

PROSCIUTTO is an Italian ham sliced paper thin and eaten as is, or fried until crisp then crumbled over food as a garnish.

RADICCHIO is a bitter Mediterranean salad ingredient. It resembles a red cabbage, with purple leaves and cream-coloured ribs. It can be used raw or cooked. Witlof, rocket or curly endive can be used instead.

ROCKET is a salad leaf popular in the Mediterranean. It has a peppery, slightly bitter taste. Small rocket leaves are often labelled as 'wild rocket' and have a stronger flavour.

SESAME OIL is a rich, brown, nutty oil made from sesame seeds. Used in Asian cooking and salad dressings, it can be found in the Asian food section at supermarkets.

SHICHIMI SEASONING (also known as *nanami tōgarashi*) is a common Japanese spice mixture made of ground red chilli, to which a variety of other ingredients have been added (typically mandarin peel, sesame seeds, poppy seeds, hemp seeds and seaweed).

SHISO is a purple or dark-green Japanese herb sometimes included in Asian salad mixes.

SICHUAN PEPPER is a red-brown peppercorn with a mouth-tingling, mildly numbing pepperiness. Used in Chinese and Japanese cooking, it is available where Asian spices are sold. Grind peppercorns finely before use. Red peppercorns can be used instead.

TAHINI (also known as sesame paste) is a creamy, dry-textured paste made from ground sesame seeds. Mixed with water and lemon juice, it is used to make salad dressings with a creamy texture and nutty flavour.

TAMARIND CONCENTRATE is a tangy, ready-to-use seasoning with a distinctive sharp lemony flavour. Available at Asian groceries, it keeps indefinitely in the refrigerator. Substitute lemon juice if necessary.

TATSOI is a small-leaf Chinese vegetable with dark round leaves on cream or green stems. It is used as a salad ingredient and is often included in Asian salad mixes.

WITLOF is a pale yellow-green or purple-red salad vegetable with crisp, tightly packed pointed leaves, with creamy-white ribs and base. Slightly bitter in taste, it is used fresh or cooked. It is sometimes also known as endive.

YAM BEAN is a root vegetable with beige skin and fluted edges. It has crisp white flesh with a taste somewhere between raw potato and apple. It is eaten raw, sliced or shredded into salads. Readily available in Asian stores. Asian pear or green apple can be used instead.

Conversions

OVEN TEMPERATURES

Celsius	Fahrenheit
180°C	360°F
190°C	375°F
200°C	390°F
220°C	430°F
240°C	465°F

WEIGHTS

Grams	Ounces
50 g	2 oz
100 g	3½ oz
150 g	5 oz
200 g	7 oz
250 g	9 oz
300 g	10½ oz
350 g	12 oz
400 g	14 oz
450 g	16 oz (1 lb)
500 g	1 lb 2 oz
600 g	1 lb 5 oz
700 g	1 lb 9 oz
900 g	2 lb

LIQUIDS

Cups/spoons	Millilitres	Fluid ounces
1 teaspoon	5 ml	⅕ fl oz
1 tablespoon	20 ml	¾ fl oz
¼ cup	60 ml	2 fl oz
⅓ cup	80 ml	2¾ fl oz
½ cup	125 ml	4½ fl oz
1 cup	250 ml	8 fl oz

SIZES

Centimetres	Inches
1 cm	⅖ in
1.5 cm	⅗ in
2 cm	⅘ in
2.5 cm	1 in
3 cm	1⅕ in
4 cm	1⅗ in
5 cm	2 in
6 cm	2⅖ in
8 cm	3 in
10 cm	4 in
12 cm	5 in
15 cm	6 in

Index

PENGUIN BOOKS

Published by the Penguin Group
Penguin Group (Australia)
250 Camberwell Road, Camberwell, Victoria 3124, Australia
(a division of Pearson Australia Group Pty Ltd)
Penguin Group (USA) Inc.
375 Hudson Street, New York, New York 10014, USA
Penguin Group (Canada)
90 Eglinton Avenue East, Suite 700, Toronto, Canada ON M4P 2Y3
(a division of Pearson Penguin Canada Inc.)
Penguin Books Ltd
80 Strand, London WC2R 0RL England
Penguin Ireland
25 St Stephen's Green, Dublin 2, Ireland
(a division of Penguin Books Ltd)
Penguin Books India Pvt Ltd
11 Community Centre, Panchsheel Park, New Delhi – 110 017, India
Penguin Group (NZ)
67 Apollo Drive, Rosedale, North Shore 0632, New Zealand
(a division of Pearson New Zealand Ltd)
Penguin Books (South Africa) (Pty) Ltd
24 Sturdee Avenue, Rosebank, Johannesburg 2196, South Africa

Penguin Books Ltd, Registered Offices: 80 Strand, London, WC2R 0RL, England

First published by Penguin Group (Australia), 2009

10 9 8 7 6 5 4 3 2 1

Text and photographs copyright © Penguin Group (Australia) 2009

Many thanks go to Freedom Furniture in South Yarra, Dinosaur Designs in South Yarra and Market Import in
Armadale, who provided a selection of the beautiful props. Thanks also to Mecca Bros Fruit City in Clifton Hill for
their wonderful produce.

The Cattivo Salted Ricotta & Broccolini Orecchiette Salad on page 179 is reproduced with kind
permission of Martin Postregna, chef and owner of Cattivo café in Camberwell, Victoria.

Cover and text design by Marley Flory © Penguin Group (Australia)
Photographs by Julie Renouf
Food styling by Lee Blaylock
Typeset by Post Pre-press Group, Brisbane, Queensland
Scanning and separations by Splitting Image P/L, Clayton, Victoria
Printed and bound in China by Everbest Printing Co. Ltd

National Library of Australia
Cataloguing-in-Publication data:

Passmore, Jacki
Salad Bible
ISBN 978 0 14 300928 3 (pbk.)
Includes index
1. Salads

641.83

penguin.com.au